FIRE
YOUR
PUBLICIST

ED ZITRON

THE PR AND PUBLICITY SECRETS THAT WILL MAKE YOU AND YOUR BUSINESS FAMOUS

For information about this title or to order other books and/or electronic media, contact the publisher:
Sunflower Press
1161 Mission Street
San Francisco, CA 94103

ISBN: 978-0-9896080-6-0 (Hardcover)
          978-0-9896080-5-3 (Softcover)

Printed in the United States of America
Cover and Interior design: 1106 Design

Dedicated to Mitch Broughton

"I'm sorry, boy. The world *needs* a generalist
but wants and is willing to pay for a specialist."

Jan 1, 1948–Oct 6, 2013

table of contents

Chapter 5—Media Preparation and Crisis Communications

foreword

When a mutual acquaintance informed me that Ed wanted me to write the foreword for his new book, at first I was confused. I knew Ed vaguely from a couple news stories in the tech world, primarily his updog prank at CES, which you'll read about later in the book (I, personally, would have asked if the companies the PR people represented were in compliance with BOFA, but that's because I am an uncultured savage and Ed is a gentleman of exquisite learning), and I didn't really understand why someone regarded as one of the best PR individuals in the industry would want an ex-NFLpunter to introduce his work.

(For those unfamiliar with American football, for most people the position of punter commands respect barely above that due the waterboy, and in many cases, less, as the quarterback will actually talk to the waterboy on occasion.)

Then I read Ed's book, and it all made sense.

You see, this book concisely lays out why, if you want to succeed in building relationships with people (since—spoiler alert—that's the literal definition of PR), it's so important to be a human being, instead of a soulless, buzzword-spewing corporate PRbot, and it's something I never really thought about before, because I thought that was simply how people were supposed to act. As someone who has built a fairly decent Twitter following (~190k people) and a fairly sizeable media presence primarily through speaking out in favor of LBGTQ rights when that was not a popular stance to take in the NFL, reading Ed's lessons on how to do PR right was like looking back at everything I had accomplished and going "Oh, so *that's* why it all worked."

Being honest. Interacting with people like human beings, not as consumers to sell something to. Making sure you care about the subjects you're addressing, and being able to relay that information quickly and accurately. Not being afraid to admit to a mistake, and apologizing meaningfully while taking steps to correct the problem. Recognizing the goal you're trying to achieve, and who is best suited to relay that message to the people you want to hear it.

These are all things I did without ever consciously thinking about them, because treating other people like actual people seemed like the right thing to do, and is, at its core, what this book is about.

You don't have to lie to sell a product, and as Ed explains, lying is actually the last thing you want to do, because it always comes back to bite you in the ass. You don't have to overwhelm some poor reporter with nonsense jargon, because that's not how real people talk to each other. You don't have to blast spam across multiple social networks, because that's not social at all, and no one is going to care.

Above all, you don't have to waste money on people who tell you to do these things, because this book gives you the tools to recognize the bullshit for what it is, and how to relate to people in a way that really matters—both for them, and for you.

To Ed—I salute you in your quest to clean up the world of PR. At the end of the day, no matter what we're trying to sell, represent, or manage, we're all human beings, and hopefully this book helps more people realize that.

To the reader—buckle up, enjoy the ride, and never let the sizzle obscure the sausage.

— Chris Kluwe

Updog certified, BOFA compliant, professional troublemaker and raconteur

(Additionally: Activist and Former NFL player)

foreword

First things first, Ed Zitron is an enigma. He is a unique riddle that you want to solve but you truly can't. You can only marvel as you read his words, listen to him, follow him and learn from him but the beauty is, that you can never really know when and how 'the dots' will connect. In actuality, you can never figure him out completely and that is the beauty of Ed, as it is with all "artists". Ed is a true artist and I'm happy to have had the honor of watching him, both up close and from a far. Either way it doesn't really matter, Ed will always take you on a wonderful trip into the unknown; Screw destination. Knowledge comes to the traveler.

Welcome to this journey!

— Peter Stormare

acknowledgments

- **Kay and Jeff Zitron,** my parents, who have supported every effort I've ever made, including some immensely stupid ones but also some of the best.
- **Royal Hebert,** my chief of staff at EZPR. He has been unstoppably supportive, insanely intuitive, and simply wonderful, not just as someone organizing my life, but as someone creating the backbone of an agency I didn't know I was capable of making as successful as it is.
- **Matt Zitron,** my brother. He consistently talked to me every single day I wrote this book, making sure I wasn't going insane (usually referring to work and my life in general).
- **Veronica Silva,** I love you, and I'm sorry I was such a grumpy bastard writing this and in general.
- **Phil Broughton,** my best friend and biggest champion in life, even when I'm far from easy to be around, and the man who taught me how to make a Manhattan.
- **Austin K. So,** my attorney. He's been a great friend, and he's stopped me from making many stupid *legal* decisions.
- **Dylan Love,** who supported me in writing this book, in writing more and in not giving up at the times I wanted to, and who made me laugh at things I didn't know I'd ever laugh at.

- **Chris Velazco,** who despite being anywhere from Hong Kong to New Jersey, seems to always be there to make me laugh at the stupidest things possible and listen to my sad ramblings at the worst times in my life.

- **Kevin Raposo,** who joined my agency as support staff and has worked harder than anyone I've ever met in PR to become better than anyone I can hire in PR.

- **Jason Lemkin,** a client who has both been wonderful to work with and an amazing mentor and educator.

- **Jon Hendren,** the creator of DevOps.

- **Zack Whittaker,** someone who has more times than I can remember pulled me out of bad psychological and written holes, and been an adoring and caring friend I'm unworthy of. He's also a very good writer.

- **Jeb Lund,** an unbelievably talented man who has advised me and listened to my personal and professional sorrows and, despite my flakiness, always been there for me.

- **Arthur Adams and Joyce Chin,** who are both amazing artists and inspirations to me and who also happen to be warm and lovely people.

- **Derek Kreindler,** the poor soul who had to edit this book, doing so with a smile and a pat on the back each time I wrote something clever.

- **Owen Williams,** who started off as a friend through work but who has become one of the best friends I've been lucky enough to have in my life.

- **Matt Weinberger,** a brilliant mind and a brilliant friend, with a similar cadence of thought and love for comics, and someone who will never turn me away at any time. My main dogg, for life.

- **Warren Ellis,** who inspired me as a writer and as someone to work with, who created some of the best things I've ever read, and who is simply a bloody good friend.
- **Chris Nicholson,** one of the most fantastic PR people I've ever met, an erudite and empathetic friend, and a hilarious man.
- **Karen Auby,** someone who despite working with me many times has remained a friend, an ally, and a great person.
- **Sheri Howell,** a friend who has done so much for me, for literally nothing, that I will never be able to repay her.
- **Peter Stormare,** a genius and one of the greatest actors I've ever seen, someone I am lucky enough to call a friend and ally.
- **Eric Nelson,** who despite never having met me, and not having any reason to, has constantly given me advice and feedback.
- **Chris Kluwe,** for introducing me to the BOFA compliance program.

introduction

In 2008, I started in public relations and left behind a career that used to make me happy on a daily basis. I used to review video games for a living.

But I had grown weary of London's weather and wanted to try living in New York. I also wanted to make more money. I'd read many books about public relations and I figured, *How hard could it be to pitch stories for a living?* I'd already been writing for years. I could easily make the switch.

I ended up joining an agency that would teach me quite quickly that the world of PR is entirely broken. "Broken" in the sense that it is a multibillion-dollar industry built on the backs of people doing the wrong thing, repeatedly. These people—through the very books that I'd read and a general lack of public knowledge of the process—had found a way to charge thousands of dollars for typing a bunch of nonsense and hitting one button.

I began to question why I'd ever left my old career, until I realized that I still needed to do PR—I just needed to do it my way.

In 2012, I founded my own agency. I'd met lots of agencies along the way that simply spammed reporters and hoped that something would stick. Somehow, at a young age, I'd become better at my job—measured by actual results, which is how one should be judged—than competitors with agencies a hundred times my size. In 2014 I was named the seventh-best PR person in technology—above the heads of PR for Microsoft and Samsung—and was profiled by *Forbes* and *Newsweek*. I started commanding tens of thousands of dollars a month. Three months into the next year, I began working with a Fortune 75 company that I'd idolized since the age of 10, hired a staff that I was proud of and adored, and wrote a best-selling book that for a few days out-sold self-improvement and leadership guru Dale Carnegie and influential investor Ben Horowitz.

In May 2015, I finished writing down exactly what I did on a daily basis. The result of that experiment is what you're reading now: this book.

I do not believe that public relations or publicity is black magic. I do believe there are so-called professionals who are not very good at their jobs and who want you to keep thinking that there's some great unknowable mystery to the work they do all day.

In this not-so-humble book, I want to do away with that. By writing this, I hope to dispel some common misconceptions about media and public relations. I hope it will be applicable whether you're a publicist, an entrepreneur or small-business owner, or just someone who wants to get noticed in this strange world.

I also spend this book referring to "being in PR." This doesn't mean you have to actually work in public relations, nor do you even have to have much interaction with the industry. More than likely, you are a person who has been or will be in PR-related *situations*, ones where you will have either hired or been the PR person.

Perhaps you'll read this book and then look at the agency or person you hired to make you famous who has failed at that task.

Perhaps then you'll make the decision that you should, indeed, fire your publicist.

PR Is Broken: Your Efforts Don't Have to Be

A cursory search of LinkedIn will show that there are more than *three million* public relations professionals in the United States. By writing this book, I hope that you'll never have to hire any of them again. If you're relying on one of these people for your publicity strategy and management right now, then I hope that you'll feel confident enough to fire them.

All right, perhaps that's a tad harsh.

But of those three million people on LinkedIn, I'd say that, at my most conservative estimate, 70 percent of them are not good. These are people who oftentimes give advice that you, as an entrepreneur, as a PR professional, as a *person*, blindly accept. It's not great advice, either. In fact much of the PR content online obfuscates and confuses situations that do not need obfuscation or confusion. PR is just not that complex. There are also many PR people and agencies that will charge you from $2,000 to $20,000 (if not more) a month, on a three-month retainer, for what is effectively a spam campaign.

Public relations is not some kind of intimidating, mystical black art that can be practiced only by attractive social butterflies. It's got nothing to do with terms such as "thought leadership," "brand engagement," "relationship management," or any of that other nonsense. PR is exactly what its name suggests—a way of relating to the public and of telling your story or the story of your brand, product, or service in a way that strikes a chord with a group as small as a few people or as big as an entire country, in the hopes that a few of those folks will have a favorable opinion of you and, in turn, pay money for whatever it is that you are selling.

If you're thinking that this sounds a bit oversimplified, well, you're right. It is. Public relations only seems complicated because there are plenty of people out there who are, for lack of a better word, charlatans. They are very charming, they make you feel good about them and their service, and they promise all kinds of access and connections and coverage in brand-name media outlets, but they don't do dick for you. They are excellent at making you feel intelligent for hiring them (or stupid for not hiring them); they are the tailors of the emperor's new clothes. And to paraphrase a menswear catch phrase of my youth, you're not gonna like what you see—I guarantee it.

My goal here is simple: to pull back the curtain on public relations. I don't care about selling you my services. (If you like what I have to say, I'm easy to find.) At the very least, I want to take a swing at laying out the basic principles for which PR firms will charge anywhere from $2,000 to $20,000 a month.

With the help of this book, I will show you how to design and execute your own public relations strategy, no matter what kind of business you are in. Forget what you think you need or what others have said are essential services. I will tell you what has worked for me and explain how you can achieve some of the same results. My goal here is to stick a dirty shiv in the backs of those who would make this overly complex for the sake of keeping PR an opaque and obscure field.

I'll walk you through the tactics and strategies you'll need to succeed in telling the world your story, and I want you to feel comfortable handling this area of your business. I want to give you the so-called secrets I have learned—as someone who fell into the industry a bit by accident and who made and endured the fallout from every mistake there is to make. You can read that story in my first book, *This Is How You Pitch: How to Kick Ass in Your First Years in PR.*

What I Do in This Book

I teach you how PR works, what agencies and PR people are really like, how to pitch media outlets, and what tools you should be using to get your message out. You can still hire an agency, and I don't even necessarily believe that you need to map and execute your entire PR strategy without input or help. But I do want you to walk into the world knowing as much as possible and thus be able to find someone who can help you accomplish your basic publicity goals with as little hassle as possible.

If you hire an agency or handle part of your own publicity strategy, I want you to feel empowered rather than uncertain or confused, and to understand basic objectives, tasks, and what to quantify in order to measure your own success, as well as that of the person or agency you hire.

A lot of PR people do not like my approach and will not like it if you are empowered by what I've written and question their authority. More than likely, they will say bad things about this book (and about me) if you ever ask them about it. Options may include:

- "Ed's an asshole."

- "Ed just wants you to buy his book."

- "Ed has an agenda."

- "Ed's a vindictive son of a bitch."

But as I bet you can guess, I don't care. I've encountered enough inept publicists and impotent agencies that don't do anything for their clients, and I think it's time that you take responsibility for your own public relations strategy and results. The goal is for you to be able to execute on the information I've laid out before you—or, at the very least, to find the right person to do so for you.

If you still need help with that last part, you can email me: ed@ezpr.com. I might not be able to help you, but I can certainly find you someone who can.

what is public relations *really* about?

CHAPTER 1

When I began my odyssey into the public relations industry, I remember thinking it was the start of something beautiful and glamorous. Instead of sitting behind a monitor typing words all by myself, as I had during my career as a games reviewer, I'd be out hobnobbing with interesting members of the media, technology, and business worlds. I assumed, based on the PR books I'd read, that I would be working with high-profile clients, helping them get A-list media coverage in top outlets, helping them plan crisis communications strategies, and attending all kinds of parties with top-shelf liquor and an open bar. This was a perception that was drilled into me through the media and through influential books written by top PR professionals, some of whom I've worked for. They talked of grandiose campaigns and wrote in aggrandizing prose about their own brilliant ideas. I believed I was to become one of those charismatic, rich, well-loved people.

Boy, was I wrong.

There are very few jobs that won't leave a coddled college graduate in a state of disillusionment, but I remember my first days in PR as a brutal grind: endless days of spreadsheets, cold-calling, and emailing people who didn't want to hear from me and didn't care what I had to say.

I remember editing documents that I knew were useless and would never be read by the smart reporters I wanted to reach. I remember sending hundreds of form-pitched emails. I remember writing press releases that I knew my boss would immediately trash because my work wouldn't conform to "the PR style," which usually meant my releases didn't include awful, made-up words like "automagically." I remember the sigh, the echo, the intonation of every forced cold-call I made. I remember every annoyed *tsk* and mean comment from a reporter I'd been instructed to call. I remember managers telling me to "get results" with no support or guidance or training to get those sought-after results.

I remember going home and crying. I remember my job being threatened because I wasn't performing up to my manager's standards. I remember every cruel word said to me: every time I was told I was stupid, every time I was told I was a bad writer, every time I was told I wasn't "getting the media to do what the client wanted." I remember every time I did my job correctly and got results—and someone else took credit for those results because he was my manager. I remember every fiber of my being telling me that calling reporters repeatedly was a bad thing and that using made-up words and overly complex jargon was a bad idea, and then being forced to ignore that instinct lest I lose my job.

I remember this because that's what this industry really is. A PR agency is cheap to establish and oversee and is a great way to produce high-margin, low-cost work.

Since my first book came out, I've heard hundreds of people echo these statements. This is the norm. This is how the industry is done at a grand scale—a boiler-room mentality of smiling, dialing, and pushing non-stories at reporters. There are good agencies, for sure.

There are many more thousands of bad agencies, including large, hulking juggernauts with hundreds of millions of dollars in retainers. You shouldn't be fooled into hiring a bad one and spending your hard-earned money on their outrageous (yet what they swear are critical) fees.

There are many obvious reasons why many professionals fall into public relations. Industry-wide, the jobs pay pretty well. Being good at being a publicist is rarely (and barely) defined. You can get a PR job almost anywhere. There will always be clients in some sort of industry that matches your interests. And it's "a great way to meet people," as you'll often be told. And to be sure, you'll meet people—if your definition of "people" is "a warm body" and not "someone you want to speak to again."

The public also has very little understanding of what public relations actually *is*. It's hard to nail down, and that's what makes it so utterly profitable for the smart-talking unethical armies of PR agencies. This leads young minds (some good ones, sadly) into a corrupt field with little or no understanding of the industry.

The education system isn't helping. College courses on PR build a perception that you will be important. A star. That you'll organize parties. That you'll lead press conferences. That you'll do things for clients that matter. That in times of crisis, you will be the one to save the day. That you'll be such an integral, important part of their world. That you will be just so smart. That your job will just be writing the occasional press release or perhaps an email, or training them because you are so smart and somehow know more about their business than they do and somehow understand how to get the press to love it. That the press wants to hear from PR people, that they're just waiting for that call. The repetition of "you're so smart" is necessary, because if you were to think for a second about what you were learning, you'd realize how utterly basic it is.

These courses fail to discuss pitching, which is the single most important element of PR. A colleague of mine told me that there wasn't a single pitching class in the four years of her public relations degree. You literally cannot do your job as a publicist without knowing how to pitch, but somehow thousands of people graduate from PR courses every year without ever learning this essential skill. Imagine if doctors went through medical school without ever learning how to take somebody's pulse. Imagine if a quarterback were never told that he had to throw *to* the wide receivers. Sounds ridiculous, right?

Now imagine an entire communications industry built on paper-thin promises and flimsy releases. Imagine an entire professional sector made up almost entirely of amateurs. You can hate the individual players if you want, but I am here to tell you to hate the game. And once you do, I am here to tell you to get in the game and make it yours to win.

I wrote this entire book knowing that the many so-called champions of industry will fight me every step of the way. They already have. I receive daily hate mail telling me that what I'm doing is wrong. Fellow publicists often tell me that it is unethical to say that there is a significant issue with the way we do business and that we are morally and ethically corrupt for forcing unnecessary, expensive services on our clients. I've been chastised for publicly explaining that it's crucial to know reporters personally and to never cold-call them—which, in addition to being a good business practice, is also commonsense etiquette.

I have tried to write this for the general public as well as for my fellow publicists. To my fellow flacks, I say again: This isn't the hardest job in the world. We work in an industry that's scamming at scale, unglamorous on a daily basis, and deeply repetitive.

Honestly, I do not know why so many publicists avoid talking about how grating and brutal the industry is, and how incompetent we are as a collective profession. For those who still haven't realized these truths, I hope this is a horrific book to read.

If you're a public relations professor reading this and disagreeing, here is a judgment aimed at you personally: You are failing your students. You are failing your academic institution, and you are a failure as an academic. You are actively sending unprepared students into a hostile, brutal industry that will cut them down and cause them great anxiety and self-loathing. You are among the few people who could have prevented that. You and I will always have a problem.

Of the however-many PR firms out there, far too many are appallingly inept. They are sending out form pitches or mail merges, which are really just elegant ways of saying that they are spamming, amounting to 50 to 100 emails each day, maybe more. They're throwing brands wrapped in crap at the wall in the hope that something will stick. This is the sole product of their work. This is what they do. This is the supposed service for which you are paying a four- or five-figure retainer. Let me spell it out: *These types of agencies and individuals are not outliers. They are the norm.* Don't believe me? Ask any reputable reporter. Writers are subject to a constant deluge of email to both their professional and personal inboxes. Most of it comes from publicists. Almost all of it is some form of professionally packaged spam.

You've probably seen a version of this sort of thing even if you aren't a journalist. You signed up to Groupon. You signed up to Nordstrom's newsletter. You signed up to a bunch of offers and lists, and it takes more effort to unsubscribe than to simply hit "delete." Imagine that people were *paid thousands to send you those uncreative blasts, and that if you opened and wrote about the contents, they'd continue to get paid.* Imagine if you could not unsubscribe. Imagine if the offers and emails only multiplied by the day.

If you happen to receive press releases, then you probably know it's commonplace to read releases that lack cohesive thought. Most releases are also incorrectly targeting the wrong writers because the publicists don't take the time to learn reporters' habits and interests and to know what would appeal to specific writers. It's sad that these types of publicity campaigns—the ones with poorly written releases sent to dozens of uninterested recipients—are still *better than the norm.* Perhaps even more horrifying is that this approach can still yield major coverage in an A-level national or international publication.

Publicity agencies offer other services, but let me be blunt: Media hits are pretty much the only reliable way to quantify PR, and publicists are half-assing the one part of their job that absolutely matters, both to the client and as a matter of industry standard. Aside from a massive conglomerate, corporation, or politico hiring a crack in-house team to handle crises, media coverage is the end game for pretty much any modern-day publicist sending out email blasts and bothering reporters.

The best publicists can write full, coherent sentences and keep track of individual writers' beats and interests. Let me repeat that: *the best publicists excel at this basic, ground-level professional etiquette and communication.* What, then, are the rest of the industry players doing? And why, then, can't everyday people do it for themselves?

Why This Book Is So Important (to Me, and to the World)

I want to be clear about something: By writing this book, I am effectively giving you the keys to my kingdom. These are trade secrets that I've learned through years of late nights at the office, missed family events, broken social engagements, and failed relationships. You could theoretically use these tricks to become me on some level. But there's a reason I'm giving it all away. To me, it goes beyond notoriety or fame or money.

It's important to know that the following is the inside baseball of the PR trade. It's stuff you might not need to know, but if you've ever hired a PR firm, you're going to be upset or know it's already happened: that you've spent your money on services rendered poorly, if at all.

There are agencies—giant, multimillion-dollar agencies—that do terrible work. They take tens of thousands of dollars and do next to nothing with it. They hand off work to their least capable junior employees and instruct them to blast hundreds of spam emails to people they do not know in the hopes that it will yield media coverage. They create pretty but useless reports that vaguely intimate that they've done enough to justify whatever exorbitant retainer they demand. They create media lists that suggest they know all the important people in an industry. All they really know is an email address. And oftentimes a publicist will find the wrong person at the wrong outlet for a story that doesn't fit—because that poor, untrained individual doesn't know how to pitch.

If you're completely outside the media ecosystem, a pitch is an email that a hopeful publicist sends to a reporter. A good pitch includes basic details about the publicist's client and perhaps a story idea, and ideally, said pitch will persuade a reporter to write about the client or the client's industry.

The absolute best way to do it, as I'll break down, is to craft and send each pitch separately, quickly, efficiently, and casually. (Note that I did not include the word "intelligently.") The problem with sending dozens of individual pitches is that it requires research, thought, *actual knowledge of an industry,* and all sorts of other troublesome work. Instead, publicists often put together a hodgepodge of buzzwords, create a mail merge (that is, connect a text document to a spreadsheet of names and email addresses), and send the same email to 100 people. Instead of taking five minutes per email, they just spent five minutes doing that a hundred times. *Kampai!* Low-quality, high-spread firing of ill-conceived, poorly targeted pitches.

Occasionally, that method is effective. And when these form pitches—so brazen, so obvious in their laziness—come across reporters' or fellow publicists' desks, we are slow to call them out. We won't use individual names; we won't use agency names. We won't say, for example, "Rogers and Cowan, an international agency comprising hundreds of people, sends mail merges that contain legitimately bad pitches." This isn't libel, by the way. I'm looking at six ridiculous releases from this exact firm from one search of my personal inbox, including two releases for fantastic companies that are clearly wasting money by retaining such an overvalued firm.

As a former journalist, I'm still the recipient of a lot of those types of email blasts. In August 2014, I received a horrific pitch about some sort of security accelerator. The messy release contained typos and buzzwords such as "innovative" and "disruptive." The author had misspelled one of the company's partner's names. And I was exactly the wrong target for this sort of thing. I don't write about security, and I never have. I also don't write about companies, unless it's for my *Inc.* column.

So I put it up on Twitter. I blacked out the names of the client and anything identifiable. A number of reporters laughed at the tweet because I added funny annotations.

Then, the agency in question emailed me and asked me to take it down because it was "causing unnecessary drama," and offered, "We will remove you from our pitch list if you'd like."

What the blue brazen hell? They'd remove me from their list if *I'd* like (as in, they still didn't realize I was a totally stupid target)? And they suggested I should delete the tweet because it was causing "unnecessary" drama? Guess what? This is necessary drama. This 11- to 50-person company charges clients a lot of money. The agency then turns around and form-pitches people with no interest or connection to the story. And the pitch was sloppy, amateur work. To me, this is *necessary drama* in the same way that if you order a pizza and it's covered in ants, you would probably be understandably upset. By all means, I am glad I threw a grenade into a client relationship. I am glad that a client, at the very least, knows the quality of an agency's supposed product.

Why does nobody else willingly call people out?

Because we are afraid of being savaged by our peers. Because perhaps we are, in aggregate, awful people doing an awful job. If we aren't mail merging, we are harassing reporters until they break and write the story. "Call the reporter until they say yes," was what one former boss told me. Many PR people still follow this maxim. *Most* do. And they justify it by saying, "It's worked before" and "It's how you get something done." There is a consistent PR–reporter culture bordering on "no means yes," and it's deplorable.

We, the publicists, are not that skilled. We are not that amazing. We are mediocre. And to make up for our shortcomings, we lie.

What PR Firms Give You for Your Money

Let's say you're a tech startup in the San Francisco Bay Area, and you've just gotten a round of funding for $1 million. This investment has to pay for everything in your short-term strategy, from your office rent to your server costs to your catered lunches (because your employees, who are working 16 hours a day, need to eat, and having them go out for lunch means an hour or so lost)—and of course, marketing and PR costs. How in the hell are you going to get noticed in *Fast Company* and TechCrunch if you don't have anyone letting the media know you exist?

You're going to need someone who can get you media coverage, who has connections with reporters, and who is plugged into the media world, assuming you can't make the time to do it yourself. And that won't come cheap. Think $5,000 to $10,000 a month to have somebody on retainer. If you're lucky, you can find professional publicists who will do it for less—$2,500 to $4,000, perhaps—and who knows if they'll be good, but it's not impossible.

Even at the lowest end, that's a lot of money, and many people wrongly assume that paying a lot of money gets you a lot more value. If they didn't, then nobody would buy a Rolex, because a Timex does the same thing. (Well, actually a Timex tells time better, but that's another topic altogether.) But when you spend more money, you buy the perception of quality and a fancy brand name.

Let me tell you what some name-brand agencies will do with that money. We've already covered mail merging, and you can expect them to do that. They'll also offer a host of other options, many of which you are just as—if not more—capable of handling on your own, and for a fraction of the cost.

When you sign with an agency, you'll probably get sold on "social media management" and on their "in-house content guru," "editorial scheduling," and "communications calendars." All this means is that a few scruffy 20-somethings (perhaps with a senior publicist as well, if you're paying more) will sit down, write your brand's blog posts and tweets in advance, and schedule them to go out at pre-determined times. Sometimes agencies even subcontract that ghostwriting to outside writers, for yet another layer of cost.

You will then receive presentations and PowerPoint decks on so-called "engagement" and "impressions," without really understanding what kind of reach or impact the agency's work is having on your company. That's the point. "Impressions" is a meaningless metric. Random people liking your Facebook posts or re-tweeting your tweets won't necessarily convert into sales, and it sure as hell doesn't mean that anybody is actually paying attention to you or what you are trying to sell.

Even if an agency can grow your Twitter followers or Facebook fans, the actual conversions into real sales are far from the Promised Land, according to a *Wall Street Journal* article from June 2014 (http://online.wsj.com/articles/companies-alter-social-media-strategies-1403499658). The article cites a Gallup poll of more than 18,000 U.S. consumers: 62 percent said social media had absolutely no influence on their purchasing decisions. Gallup concluded, "Consumers are highly adept at tuning out brand-related Facebook and Twitter content" and ". . . social media are not the powerful and persuasive marketing force many companies hoped they would be." This study flies in the face of more than $5.1 billion spent on social-media advertising by

North American companies in 2013. It goes to show that money isn't everything. Far from it.

Unfortunately, you'd probably like to get something for your money, and often, these social media manager charlatans are getting paid handsomely to add very little value to your business. It sure is great you have all those blog posts and tweets. It's great that you have an ambitious plan to talk about things on the Internet. But little of that actually converts into gaining new customers or earning money. The PR firm or individual agency representative in question often isn't thinking of that. Or if they are, they're scared to say so because it might not be what you want to hear.

So let's get to it.

What Is Public Relations?

Contrary to what most people think, public relations has less to do with how you are *perceived by* the public than with how you *relate to* the public.

I mean, *relations* is in the bloody term, but a lot of people have understandably come to a point where they think publicity is first and foremost about manipulation.

At its most basic, public relations is about saying things in a way that everyday (if not specific groups of) people can understand. The particular group you are trying to reach can vary wildly in size and makeup. Sometimes you'll be targeting reporters that cover a certain beat, and sometimes you'll be aiming to communicate with an entire geographic region. An enterprise software executive may want to reach out to reporters covering technology and business just to get on the radar. On the flip side, an oil company dealing with a massive spill might employ a PR strategy for the region affected by the spill, or even the entire planet, in hopes of mitigating negative public perception, repairing its image, and managing media coverage. These are two very different scenarios, but both fall under the public relations umbrella.

Relating to the public is a necessity, and that means that limiting the flow of information is not what public relations is all about. Controlling it? Yes. You may have to not say certain things because you or your client cannot respond in a way that is helpful to anyone at that point in time. You may have to say, "My chief executive can't speak with the public right now," and the best course of action is to tell the truth, which is that the CEO needs to work out what is happening and get the right information to the reporter.

On the agency side, often clients want to obfuscate, withhold things, or use a playbook that some people would consider ethically dubious. This includes but is not limited to lying, lying by omission (also known as "spin"), and so-called "flipping the conversation," which means rather than answering a reporter's question—especially if it's a question for which you might have to give a negative answer—just describing something positive or telling a different story entirely. Anything for the publicity, right?

I saw a clear-cut example of latching onto a negative story for your own potential benefit in August 2014, when a publicist pitched a story that vaguely connected his client's app, Vizsafe, to the brutal treatment of peaceful protesters in Ferguson, Missouri (http://valley wag.gawker.com/tech-pr-dummies-dont-use-ferguson-to-sell-your-app-1623322180). This kind of action is unethical ambulance-chasing that seeks to make profit out of pain. When I questioned that publicist about his unquestionably gross ethics, he replied, "Look up press for client. This pitch got them on Bloomberg West. So, we good." In essence, they're good! Because they got good press results. That's how many publicists measure themselves, and they often train clients to expect the same.

No industry publication covered this poisonous, vomit-inducing response. The Public Relations Society of America (PRSA), our industry's so-called professional organization, put together a milque-toast piece (http://prsay.prsa.org/index.php/2014/08/15/friday-five-responding-after-a-tragedy/) in an attempt to tie "social media" to "police shooting at normal civilians." There was no post or statement by the organization actively decrying a practice that was at best crass and at worst wholly unethical.

PRNewser, Mediabistro's PR blog, responded in a measured way (http://www.mediabistro.com/prnewser/your-first-ferguson-pitch_b97940) but stopped short of saying, as everyone should have, "Check out this unprofessional asshole." The public relations industry is too meek in the face of unambiguous dishonesty.

Whereas there are ombudsmen in most fields to call out bad actors, we in publicity do not want to call them out. We should, but we do not. People who work in public relations, and the media as a whole, should step forward and state, "This person and this agency are doing disgraceful, disserviceable work." Hell, the *client* should fire the agency.

To be clear, there's nothing wrong with being a legitimately useful news source. If you're, say, a retired Missouri police chief or an authority on the militarization of the police, you're a good source here. Pitching yourself as an expert or having your publicist do so isn't unethical. In that case, you would not be not news-jacking. You'd be actively helping a reporter and informing the world at large.

Put simply, doing public relations properly means getting your message across in a way that people can clearly understand. That is challenging, and it won't get any easier when you are fighting an uphill battle in the arena of public opinion.

The truth is that you aren't always going to win these battles, but you can always put your best foot forward. That way, you will earn points for courage, integrity, and honesty, even if it seems like you're not getting the results you want. And you'll be doing a better job than most professionals you could have hired.

Why Am I Pulling Back the Curtain on Public Relations (and Why Are So Many Publicists So Inept)?

Simple. I think telling it like it is when it comes to PR is important because I think that a lot of public relations-related work is being done very badly, to the point where anyone (and that means you, the non-publicist reader) could do a better job without having to fork over your first-born child in retainer fees.

On a personal level, I also see a multimillion-dollar scam being perpetrated. Don't worry; this entire book isn't some sort of *Count of Monte Cristo* adventure. I just need to give you context so that you understand what's going on behind the curtain (and on the stage, too).

I am biased in the sense that I come from a technology background and have seen a lot of stuff that makes my blood boil. Sure, part of me says, "Man, I could do a better job, and I like money." But for the most part, I simply see an unethical maelstrom that is not being addressed. I want to help address it by empowering individuals and helping publicists do a better job overall.

Have you ever read a piece of copy for a startup? Do you see the same buzzwords over and over again? "Game changing," "disruptive," "innovative," and all those other flaky terms that have you wondering,

"Just what exactly does this thing do to make my life better and/or generate revenue?"

Using these fluffy words sounds great to people who either don't know better or don't want to say that the emperor is naked. But do these words really communicate to the public exactly what a business is or what service it provides?

Tech is far from the only industry that is governed by a herd mentality when it comes to PR services. Businesses grow to a certain size and think that they need someone to handle publicity for the company—and this is not incorrect. Some executives think that they need PR immediately because a competitor has a PR team or has retained an agency. One might think that hiring a huge agency is the best route to take because that agency helped ABC Big Company land tons of press. That's fine, but that sort of decision is often made without acknowledging all the facts, including that ABC Big Company has millions of dollars set aside to hire celebrities and put on high-octane events to significantly boost visibility and, perhaps eventually, attain success.

For example, social media and public relations firm SocialRadius proudly boasts that it helped earn millions of hits for world-famous musician will.i.am's award-winning "Yes We Can" video, released in support of Barack Obama's presidential nomination. It is not a challenge to make people pay attention to will.i.am, or indeed Barack Obama, even before he was president. Relying on attention-grabbing performers and politicans and a "social campaign" of this nature really requires little more than letting will.i.am just make a video. Pitching and claiming success for a campaign that would have gone viral on its own is like making a Pop-Tart correctly and claiming this achievement makes you a chef.

Executives also tend to assume that they need a blog as well as a social media strategy, and again, these are tools to have in the kit. But some folks fail to consider why they need those tools and which ones are the best to deploy to reach their goals—assuming those goals have been defined beyond "I want a Facebook page and Instagram account because all my competitors have them."

How to Spot Bad Public Relations and Publicity

If you've ever bought a used car, you know that the car dealer is basically relying on your ignorance of automobiles to try to sell you a rolling heap of crap and make a handsome profit doing so. PR isn't so different, sadly.

I don't blame the public relations industry for this. I blame humanity. Everyone, no matter how crappy, wants to be famous or well regarded. Everyone wants to sell his or her own rolling heap of crap and benefit from it.

When you are first looking for a publicist or agency to help you out, you're going to get more of the same bullshit buzzwords and empty promises from so-called full-service agencies helping to "design and execute engagement strategies with your stakeholder" and "build your brand" and whatever other nonsense people are trying to shove down your throat. The staffers at these firms often look and act the same anywhere you go—bright-eyed, bushy-tailed young professionals spitting these same words. Be assured that your investment is safe in the hands of people who don't talk like humans. They approach real-world people with this language—including reporters, who do *not* talk like this—and consistently fail to engage on a basic conversational level.

It's not their fault. Most new PR professionals are at an immediate disadvantage simply because PR-related education is subpar.

Many new publicists learn what they know from teachers who are rarely still working in the field. These instructors are often people who led PR efforts 10 or 20 years ago. They might have an agency on the side, but they aren't involved in a lot of the day-to-day stuff that keeps their knowledge and skills relevant—aspects of the job as critical as working in social media since its inception or keeping tabs on the most reputable online publications in an emerging industry. Colleges have no idea what a "good PR professional" looks like and thus hire people who have had impressive titles (for example, Director of Communications in Government X, Big Company Y, or Large Agency Z), which only means that the instructor has a very narrow skill set. Then the institution installs them to teach. For years.

The result is that new-on-the-job publicists start with a complete lack of understanding of the real world of public relations. They've been taught by professors who don't know the contemporary public relations ecosystem. They haven't been taught to pitch or even what it takes to craft an interesting story. There's no journalism training, which means that publicists who want to land media hits don't even know how reporters work, let alone what they want.

A PR instructor once told me that he spent very little time on the craft of pitching and instead told his students to learn to pitch in 75 characters or less, "because that's what social media is like." This is a great thing to say as some sort of catchphrase, but in reality there's very little you can tell someone in *literally a few words,* and he happily admitted that he didn't teach students how to write a longer pitch from which to select a few key points.

Why am I telling you this? Why do I keep harping on this point, and why does it matter so much? Because if you are hiring an agency or an individual publicist, you have to understand how you're spending your money, in the same way you'd want to make sure that you knew how a car went forward and how the brakes worked.

University instructors also don't tell you how to build a network that will help you effectively spread your message, teach you which social media tools are worth your time, or offer any of the other practical tips this book will teach you so that you get maximum results with minimum time and effort.

If you really want to get intellectual about it, PR should be looked at as *a study in warfare*. It is a battle against a united front of individuals—reporters, executives, fellow publicists, even everyday people—who hate what you do for a living and probably hate your industry even more. If you're handling publicity from within an organization, your biggest foe will often be your *own organization*. As an in-house publicist, you'll find that everybody has an opinion about how the organization should look, which publications should feature the company or founder story, and what you should say to reporters. By the end of this book, you may find those things doubly frustrating. But I hope you'll also be inspired to do your job more effectively, make it more important to your organization, and find even more value in what you do.

Why Public Relations Matters to Ordinary People

The best way to arm yourself for battle is to eliminate lazy PR practices from your own toolkit or from that of the agency you are using to do the work for you.

Here are some red flags:

- **Someone with a superficial understanding of your business and your industry.** Ideally, your PR person will be a specialist in whatever it is that you do. I specialize in tech, games, and startup PR. On an industry level, I try to keep to a reporter-level standard of industry knowledge, meaning I can speak off the cuff with informed authority on a lot of topics in the same industry. Some examples: I keep up with new releases in gaming (that is, I actually play them; I don't just know their names), and I can still build a PC. This requires an active interest in the industry and a fair amount of effort and time to maintain. I read anywhere from 30 to 50 news articles every day. It doesn't feel like work because I'm interested in it, but it is technically work. I also know the technical levels, too. I can't write code, but I know about the main spread of programming languages and the major repositories. This sounds like a boast, but it's what I consider the minimum knowledge necessary to respectfully have a discussion with a reporter.

Although I'm capable of representing a game developer or a software engineer, I wouldn't touch something in the medical field or the arts. What the hell do I know about medical devices? I certainly don't know much at all about the current state of theater, ballet, or even cinema. I also don't know about toys, fashion, or large-scale retail. These are all types of clients I'll turn down. Why? Because it'd be impossible for me to do a good job. In fact, it'd be impossible for most people to do a good job, because if you want to approach something intelligently in PR, you have to know about it well enough to explain it *correctly to a layman*.

Sadly, this runs exactly contrary to how some agencies view publicists. To some, the best publicist is a generalist and might cover a motorcycle company, a condiment maker, and a record label, having only a general understanding of these three businesses. The best PR people, who are very rare, could juggle all of these different industries and have a rock-solid understanding of all the nuances and minutiae. That's why they're the best. Most PR people aren't the best but will say that they are, even when that is impossible. You can combat this by handling your own public relations, or you could use this information when you consider hiring a publicist in the future. Is she already very well educated *or prepared to learn?* Being able to answer that one question can save you considerable costs down the line.

- **Form pitching.** In my opinion, form pitching is a cardinal sin. As I've discussed, form pitching is basically a copy-pasted email blast with only the name of the journalist changed (at best). Form pitches aren't personal, provide no value to the reporter, and are downright insulting to many writers. If you want to target the appropriate media outlets, you will have to get to know each reporter individually, learn the angles they like to cover, and tailor your pitches to them.

  Note that it can be very hard to find out if the publicist you hired is form-pitching and spamming reporters instead of cultivating relationships that will help your company story or message reach a wider audience. But it will be obvious if the publicist isn't getting results, and it wouldn't be entirely unfair to blame this on poor pitching, in either content or method. You can ask to see the pitches that are being sent out, but most likely, the publicist or agency will not share them.

If you're really worried you're wasting your money and the publicist you hired won't show you his work, you can catfish him and try to uncover what's really going on. This is a pretty extreme tactic—and you probably haven't established enough trust with the person you hired if you have to resort to this—but you can create a fake email address, pose as a freelance reporter, and ask for some pitches from the publicist. If the publicist you hired wastes time on this, he's probably wasting time on a lot of other bullshit, too. And you probably need to fire him if you're already suspicious he's wasting your time and money in such a spectacular fashion.

- **Reliance on jargon and buzzwords.** Pitches, like most interactions (especially those with reporters), should be clear, plainspoken, and honest. No one should have to dress up the facts with flowery language or jargon that makes a topic sound more important than it is. Do not pay money to have someone do this for you. Reporters, more than anyone else, appreciate honesty, candor, and an economy of language. You can charm a reporter by being a normal human being and get better results through that alone than through paying to have someone pester them to get coverage for you.

    For example, one of my clients is a service that compiles dossiers of publicly available information (from LinkedIn, for example) and provides them to salespeople, PR people and other media professionals. A PR agency of ill repute and bad English might call it an innovative way to extract data on those you're planning to engage with on a business basis. I know that my method got them The Next Web, TechCrunch, *Business Insider,* and about 10 other pieces in the first week. And that was for a product update.

- **Failing to provide real value or the deliverables that the client wants.** Or to put it another way, beware the publicist or agency that tells you, the client, what you should want rather than offering what you request and meeting your demands.

  Let's say you want coverage in a national newspaper for your new product. You need to understand that your publicist (whether that's you or someone you've hired) can't just wave a magic wand and get you the front page of the *Wall Street Journal.* Hard-working publicists will do their best to reach that goal. If they can't, they'll explain why they couldn't deliver and offer an alternative solution. They will also probably manage your expectations from the beginning, which is a crucial but often overlooked and underappreciated characteristic of truly honest, helpful publicists. If they know the media landscape well enough, they'll know which of your dreams has wings and which ones should be gracefully grounded in reality. You should not only let them tell you the difference between the two but heed the advice that sometimes, the best press you can get is from a publication you hadn't even considered on your own.

  Bad publicists will realize the magnitude of your request to be covered by the *Journal* but will lead you down several paths paved with lies. They'll say happily that this is a smart request that they can *totally handle* and that they're "making progress"—without any insight into what they're actually doing. They might tell you that a reporter "is reviewing the material," which could mean anything from knowing the email was successfully received to the reporter replying, "I'll take a look." They will string you along because you're paying them money, and they like money. Don't we all? They won't want to admit that they're actually getting nowhere—and that there's no real way of moving it along beyond mind control.

Truly unethical publicists may try to convince you that the legacy media *just isn't that important anymore*—that you don't need to bother with placements in magazines or even in web publications—and that perhaps you need to think of doing some content marketing, which is code for "Pay us more to write blogs for you." They might suggest you pay for a "tweet sponsorship package," which is when someone has a discussion on Twitter and your company pays to sponsor it. (This is a real thing that happens.) There are many methods they might suggest that aren't valuable but that make them look well connected or smart.

They're simply not listening, or even suggesting reasonable alternatives or more effective strategies. They're just trying to get you off their back by steering you toward something you can be billed for.

You're reading this book because you want to be able to distinguish the good advice (such as managing your expectations about media coverage) from the bad advice (which bullshit, vaguely trendy, or truly unproven services you should buy).

One more anecdote about unethical publicists and how to catch them in action: One time, another PR rep constantly told a client that they were "friends" with people. I was forced to work with him on said client. I actually walked out of the meeting and decided not to work with him because I found him @messaging those "friends" on Twitter, to no response.

Why the World Still Needs People Like Me

I'm sure you're wondering why someone such as myself, who makes a living from having people hire him to handle publicity, is going to divulge all the secrets and tradecraft of public relations.

It's actually pretty simple. I love PR, I love what I do, and I love my clients. I hate to see lazy, unprincipled, and incompetent publicists taking people's money for shoddy work that doesn't move the needle for anything but the publicist's bank account. I don't even necessarily want that money. I'd prefer that money not change hands at all rather than end up in the wrong ones. I want to see great companies stop spending major cash on nothing. I want the big agencies to either lose money or become better at what they claim to do.

I really do hold the firm conviction that with enough time and inclination, individuals can become effective PR people for themselves. Some people truly don't have time or affection for this sort of work, so for them it will be easier to hire a good firm to handle all the tasks. But for those of you who are OK with the DIY approach, this book will break down everything you should be doing. From content creation to social media platforms to press releases, you can learn what is required to take ownership of your publicity and reach the audience you want—without spending thousands of dollars on a few press releases and phone calls.

how to handle your own PR, and the way of the pitch

The first chapter spent a lot of time focusing on the ubiquity of ineffective public relations and why that should change. You may be surprised to learn that there are methods that work when it comes to PR, and no matter who you are, you can employ a lot of the simple tactics on your own, no agency or publicist required.

This chapter will lay it all out for you and hopefully make you examine commonplace PR strategies and tools with a more critical eye. Just because someone else has a Pinterest page or an Instagram account doesn't mean you need one, too. But a lot of agencies will gladly tell you that you do and then bill you handsomely for it. A great deal of PR comes down to earning a measurable return, versus doing something because you think you have to. Pitching a product or service is the core of what most people actually want and expect when hiring a public relations professional. The issue is that targeted pitching to receptive individuals is hard to do, and that's why I'm going to spell out exactly how to do it. Media results build, enhance, and perpetuate your reputation and product, and create an environment in which people see objective individuals (reporters, bloggers, people on social media) already discussing it.

The added bonus of knowing how to pitch is that it feeds into a great deal of other fields. In general, by learning to pitch, you'll find you're able to convincingly email people and communicate more effectively. If you're able to find that magic that turns something from dull to interesting, just imagine what it could do for your dating life!

That's a joke. Sort of. But the art of the pitch is really at the heart of how most successful people stay successful. There's a thin line between pitching and bullshit, and it exists at the point where you learn to mine for worthwhile discussion elements about any particular topic. But whether you're pitching a reporter or having a drink with a friend, don't make things up.

Before we truly begin digging into the nuances of public relations truth-telling, though, let's take a step back and look at what we are actually trying to accomplish.

Public Relations = Managing Your Reputation

In my first book, *This Is How You Pitch*, I led off with a simple explanation of what public relations is all about: managing your reputation with the public. Even if that means you're *creating* a reputation.

When you hire a publicist, you are essentially hiring somebody to manage your reputation for you. Since you're reading this book, you've decided to take it into your own hands on some level. Bravo. Unfortunately for you, you could not have picked a tougher environment.

One of the most critical parts of publicity is not the outreach but the simple, methodical building of a solid reputation—and unfortunately, there's no magic bullet for achieving one. What you can do, with the help of this book, is lay the foundation for a good reputation, each and every day, through your interactions both online and in person.

Ironically, the same environment that has allowed for a world of constant media attention is one that will allow you to take control of your reputation on your own terms—without the hassle and expense of hiring a professional. And most of the time, the very idea of *reputation* isn't even on people's radar. In fact, nobody thinks about your reputation but you. What you need to care about is the way people, on average, feel about you and how you can help change it (preferably without lying, manipulating, or being an awful human).

Why Reputation Matters

Anyone who has ever been in any sort of successful relationship—whether romantic, platonic, or strictly business—knows that trust and communication are two primary building blocks for a solid foundation. In the context of one's own publicity, communication means how you communicate with the public, and your reputation stands in for the trust element. In the same way these aspects matter in any interpersonal relationship, what you communicate to the public can be meaningless if the trust isn't there. You may not be lying when you tell your partner that you really were out at a client event and that the lipstick on your collar is the result of some unwanted attention from someone you find revolting—but if your partner doesn't trust you, no explanation in the world will mollify the hurt feelings or patch over the doubt. Trust is built on a pattern of clear, unwavering actions and through reliability and talking through things, even topics and issues that aren't necessarily fun to discuss.

Building trust through communication is not much different when it comes to public relations.

A professional reputation built on honesty can insulate you from significant failure or will at least help others give you the benefit of the doubt in most situations. If you're young or inexperienced enough to not have much of a public reputation, honesty is still the best way forward. If something goes wrong—anything from an employee posting offensive remarks on social media to your company being held responsible for an environmental disaster—being up front with customers, shareholders, and especially the public is the thing that matters most. If you aren't honest and attempt to hide your mistakes like cat turds in a litter box, things tend to go badly. All the damage control and crisis communications in the world won't help you if you already have a poor reputation.

Think about how some politicians are perceived. The nature of running for and holding public office is that some of your constituents— sometimes up to half the people you represent—won't agree with your baseline values and principles. But there's a distinct difference between being perceived as a shady, say-anything politico uninterested in public service and being a respectable, trustworthy leader on the opposite side of the ideological spectrum. The latter has a shot at holding office in almost any environment because she—specifically, her reputation—can weather a storm. Someone with a shaky moral character is less likely to have a solid reputation to lean against when a storm hits.

If you're the last to speak up when your firm or industry has a crisis on its hands, there's little you can do to stop the public from interpreting it as a cynical dodge to save your own hide. And if you're not handling the situation yourself (which I cover in later chapters), you'll be paying the biggest bucks for this kind of help.

This will sound slightly annoying, but it's true: the easiest and most typical way to avoid painful public scrutiny and professional blowback is an ironclad reputation. If you want to inoculate yourself against criticism, you should always consider how others perceive your words and actions, and how that might reflect on a product or service you want to sell.

Reputation is not the same as fame. If you're an executive or a bestselling author, you might be able to rely on a bit of both. If you're less established professionally, you can take steps as simple as joining a social network such as Twitter and befriending a few of the right people. I often advise clients that, well before their product launches or their fledgling company gets off the ground, they should start following news and reading profiles about executives in their industry, as well as working to form a relationship with reporters. Nothing will create an impenetrable force field around you if you say something truly reprehensible or your product harms half the planet. But reputation is like a cloud that surrounds you. You can have a sizable impact on your environment just by how you contribute to the atmosphere and relate to what's around you.

There may be totally unforeseen instances in which your business and livelihood are on the line, and events that were totally beyond your control threaten to turn your world upside down. Maybe you have a rogue employee who writes racist comments in public forums. Maybe your company didn't solve the problems it claimed to or obfuscated the truth in pursuit of higher profits. These types of rare instances can be dealt with individually, but even then, having a good reputation will help insulate you from the radioactive fallout that threatens to poison the way people think about you. When the media comes to you to ask questions, you don't want this to be the first time they hear about you. That's actually one of the greatest ways to start life with a bad reputation.

Take the case of the chief executive of Theranos. Months before her company's methods were called into question, many people had heard about the young, hardworking CEO behind the company promising to revolutionize blood testing. Elizabeth Holmes found herself in hot water in late 2015, when the *Wall Street Journal* questioned the methods used by her medical-testing company. But although known for being extremely private, Holmes had made public appearances and given talks about her work. She'd started to build up some goodwill before her company was cast in a shadow of doubt.

Now, many months later, her entire company has fallen apart as a result of complete lies. Calling it a house of cards is too kind. The Theranos PR strategy of complete lies is too much to dig into, but can be summarized simply.

Don't say you can do a thing you can't do, no matter how impressive it may make you seem or how attractive that lie may be.

Not only is this sort of reputation-building important for external purposes, but when everything is going to shit, you need all hands on deck. Do you think your employees will feel motivated or fired up about going to work and doing what needs to be done during a crisis if your firm is looked upon as the devil's own workshop?

It's not just rats that flee a sinking ship. Your employees have bills to pay, careers to manage, and nosey neighbors, overbearing parents, and nagging spouses. They want to show up, get paid, and not be judged or hounded about working for a company that just sent out misogynistic tweets or buried radioactive waste in the Arctic National Wildlife Refuge. It would be nice to think that they're loyal and willing to help you persevere through tough times, but that probably isn't the case. It's also important to remember that sometimes the things that go wrong are things that your employees don't know about, and thus your reputation and judgment may be vital to keeping them around.

On the other hand, if your reputation is sterling, then they'll likely have a cause to rally around. They'll feel as if they're part of a noble effort to get things back on track, rather than selling their days to the world's shittiest organization. A reputation is as much a tool for internal communications and morale building as it is for making the public think you're great.

How to Manage Your Reputation in One Easy Step

Just kidding! Nothing takes one step, except the one you take off a cliff. As I've said, there's no magic bullet for public relations, and if you find yourself needing one, it's probably too late to load the chamber.

On the other hand, it's never too late to adopt the most crucial mindset for success: every individual action you take will collectively constitute your reputation. That's not to say you can never make mistakes. But the key to establishing a positive reputation is a consistent track record of excellence, whether it involves the product, the marketing, the customer service, or even the company's public relations itself. When you think about a top-tier brand in any given marketplace, you'll see that this is a common denominator among all of them. A Rolex watch may not keep time as well as a cheap digital watch, but as a company, Rolex has done a fantastic job of cementing its reputation as the maker of the finest watches in the world. In fact, you could fill a book with examples of *how* they've managed to do this, even though a Casio G-Shock costs a fraction of the price and is technically superior. Yet the legend persists.

The opposite is true when you truly screw up in some way, shape, or form; your response to the situation will likely color your reputation forever. If you are honest and up front, even when you do something bad, it can work out. If you're duplicitous and *especially* if you're caught in a lie, your company will face a gigantic black eye.

Here's an example of how this can play out even when it seems like an individual or company long ago established a solid reputation. Lenovo, for many years, enjoyed a reputation as making quality laptops of varying prices. They had good reviews and a good reputation (especially for their ultrabooks and touch-screen laptops), and they were well respected amongst their peers, including ASUS and Dell. In fact, by May 2014 they had become the world's biggest maker of personal computers, selling 55 million PCs in a year (http://www.zdnet.com/article/lenovo-sales-55-million-pcs-50-million-smartphones-and-nine-million-tablets/). They owned nearly 20 percent of the market share and were named one of *Forbes*'s "Fab 50" Asian companies (www.forbes.com/companies/lenovo/).

In February 2015, it was discovered that on some new laptops, Lenovo had pre-installed software, called Superfish, that replaced advertisements on users' Google searches (and elsewhere) without users' permission. The online security community quickly jumped on this software when it was found to be filled with a number of potential security pitfalls (http://thenextweb.com/insider/2015/02/19/lenovo-caught-installing-adware-new-computers/). The most notable security hole meant that hackers would be able to snoop into a user's web history, including passwords, emails, and other confidential information. This software was shipped in many, many laptops, and the online security community quickly came up with many ways that this was both unethical and unsafe for users. In fact, it was actually far worse than anyone thought (www.techdirt.com/articles/20150223/07363930113/thought-komodiasuperfish-bug-was-really-really-bad-its-much-much-worse.shtml).

Lenovo's response was to declare up and down that this was a tool for discovering new products (www.wired.com/2015/02/lenovo-superfish/). When the security community continued to demand explanations, the company's chief technical officer simply said, "We messed up" (www.pcworld.com/article/2886690/lenovo-cto-admits-company-messed-up-and-will-publish-superfish-removal-tool-on-friday.html). Lenovo eventually released a tool to remove Superfish from its machines, as did several other Adware services.

I can't speak for the product cycle or for the thoughts in anyone's heads that made them install this software, and I don't know whether changing their minds would have helped them avoid a lawsuit (www .pcworld.com/article/2887392/lenovo-hit-with-lawsuit-over-superfish-snafu.html). What I can speak for is that the moment anyone said anything about Superfish, about how bad it was, the company's official response should have been something along the lines of, "This was a really bad decision on our part. We did not mean to do anyone harm. Here's our reasoning. We *did* mess up, and here's how we'll make it up to you."

This full-fledged scandal was handled in pure corporate jargonese, organized and executed with the grace and candor of a drunk elephant. Decisive, humble apologies and an immediate "Oh, wow; we messed up" may not have stopped people from being angry at Lenovo, but it might have curbed the avalanche of articles and negative tweets.

At the other end of the spectrum, we have Apple. Apple's electronics are expensive but not out of reach for the average consumer. The Apple versus PC debate is irrelevant here, and so are the hardware and design elements (though those did help the company a lot).

Where Apple has won over legions of fans is with their retail stores. I'd argue that no single element has further enhanced their reputation than a person being able to walk into any store at any time and talk to somebody who knows the product front to back. Can't figure out how to add a transition in iMovie? Lost your MacBook power supply? Is your iPod not charging properly? Drop your iPhone in the toilet? Well, guess what? You can go into a beautifully designed store stocked with enthusiastic, friendly, and knowledgeable staffers who will help remedy your problem on the spot. For a price, someone will be able to fix just about any Apple product, and they'll frown along with you at your plight.

This level of service is, in my opinion, the biggest source of Apple's bulletproof following among its fans. Every single product launch is a major event, and the company has earned this sort of coverage because its leaders focus on being excellent at each step of the way, from the design to the user experience to the sales process to the customer care package available to consumers when they buy the device. It's fair to say that people are generally thrilled with their Apple products and can't wait to buy more.

And yet the world is littered with amazing ideas, concepts, and products that never made it anywhere, and that's because there was nobody to tell the world how great they were. At a minimum, you still need to let everyone know that it exists. Otherwise, you're like the teenage wallflower at the school dance, sitting in the shadows and hoping that someone will notice how great you are.

When Apple has faced scandals, the company has faced them quickly and decisively. Its sterling, lily-white reputation has been echoed even in its crisis response. When Apple's iPhone 6 and 6+ devices launched, they were plagued by reports that the phones would bend in your pocket during average use. The media went insane over the idea that the newest, hottest phone of 2014 would curve like a reed in the wind, posting pictures and indeed trying to bend the phones themselves, at times successfully. This is because any phone that is made of aluminum will, at some point, bend. Instead of saying that people were wrong and that bending didn't occur, Apple representatives admitted that nine reports of bent phones had been confirmed and that the company would replace any bent phones that passed a visual inspection (http://www.pcmag .com/article2/0,2817,2469324,00.asp). They also made it clear that there were normal ways to use a phone (such as not sitting on it for 18 hours) and that if the phone did unintentionally bend, Apple would replace said phone. The end.

So-called "Bendgate" remains a joke, a reminder that even the great Apple can experience imperfections. What Apple didn't bend was the truth; the company acknowledged how many requests it had received for repairs and set up an official policy for fixing it—and quickly, too. The Apple name and reputation, unsurprisingly, has not slowed down the sales of the latest (at the time of this writing) iPhone.

Now that you understand a little bit more about what a reputation is, can be, or can be reduced to, you may want to know how to create, maintain, and sustain one.

The Perks of Being a PR Maverick

If you've never hired a PR agency before, here's what's dangerously likely to happen.

You'll send an email to whatever firm you want to speak to. You'll get on a call with a couple of agency representatives, and they'll express excitement over the potential opportunities they have to take your money. You'll meet with employees, some of whom will probably have a title like "Vice President" or "Account Director" or something important sounding. Whether they're male or female is irrelevant. They'll probably be attractive and charming, and they'll make you think they're interested in you by saying nice things about you and your business. They'll come up with wild and fanciful ideas for you, depending on how much money you have to burn, ranging from "trends" you fit into to potential "event ideas," most of which are very loosely connected to reality.

None of it will mean very much at all.

They most likely won't get to know you, your employees, your industry, your market segment, your product, your corporate culture, or any of the unique things that make your organization what it is. What they will do is potentially charge you a ton of money every month for doing abhorrently lazy things like creating standardized emails via a mail merge, which, as I've covered, is basically an Excel Spreadsheet of reporter names and contact details mated to a template email in Outlook. One click sends it out to everyone on the list—mainly, to reporters who have no interest in you. This might yield some results. It probably won't.

This isn't to say all agencies are bad. Indeed, there are some fantastic publicists and agencies out there. The problem is with the word "some." Many multimillion-dollar (and hundred-million-dollar) agencies still effectively spam reporters and retain major contracts with major industry clients (Microsoft, for example), which means that even if the agency does nothing of actual value, reporters are still forced to bother with this middleman.

If you aren't the Microsoft equivalent of your industry segment and you've hired a publicist, well, I suggest you read your contract. It likely promises nothing. No return on investment, no results, no media coverage, no measurable way to quantify the services for which you have paid. Does that mean the agency won't deliver on anything its publicists have promised? I have seen it happen, and I won't bore you with more details.

Now you may see why I am so keen to promote do-it-yourself publicity or, at the very least, knowing what to expect and how to prevent being completely ripped off by a publicist who assumes you don't know much about what they promised to deliver.

The One Thing You Need to Know to "Do Good PR": The Pitch

One thing is so crucial to PR that I put it in a book and say it far too many times a day. It's the thing that will get you business, get you noticed, get a number, or potentially get you out of trouble.

It's called pitching.

Pitching has many contexts. If you're a business owner, startup founder, or creative professional, you've pitched something before, even if you don't know it. If you have had an idea for a business, you've probably pitched an investor. If you are a freelance journalist, you've definitely pitched an article or subject to an editor (and likely to a PR person). The problem with the concept is that many people see it in the realm of being a salesperson.

Yes, of course you want to persuade someone to do something: hire you, talk to you, invest in your company. But some of the finest pitches are done based not on hyperbole but on the raw truth.

In the context of public relations, pitching is getting someone to talk or write about you, your product, your service, or whatever it is that you're selling. (Even if you run a nonprofit and do not technically sell anything, this still applies.)

When you pitch, the most important thing you can do—and it's a thing that most PR pros fail to do—is find a square hole for your square peg. That is, you need the right pitch for the subject, and you need to pitch it to the right people. I hate to say it, and many will disagree with me, but there are some products, people, and things that simply do not fit into some areas. Some people and businesses simply won't be profiled or featured in certain publications. PR firms (and general day-to-day morons) may promise, "Oh, yeah—you're totally gonna be in the *New York Times* in your first month," but if that person doesn't understand both you and the media market, he's making a promise that he can't keep.

The truth is that this is also important information for you, dear reader. If you do indeed retain a publicist, you need to understand the reality of the media landscape, as well as the wider world. This means that if you're made a fanciful, unproven promise, you should understand that it's not possible. Conversely, even if it's true, it may be months or years before you hit the hallowed pages of the *New York Times* or other world-renowned outlets.

I know from experience that not everyone wants to hear this. Fun story: I lost my job at a home improvement social network for posting your projects you're working on the day after telling my boss, two months into the job, that the company would not be in the *New York Times* for a long time. The company site was buggy, the spokesperson was, frankly, just not that interesting to talk to or particularly likeable, and the product was not different enough from the competition.

Telling my boss the truth and losing my job over it sucked, but I'm glad I was fired, because working with that team and product further would have meant more conversations where I had to tell them about a reality no one wanted to face. It also helped me decide to start my own agency, which I suppose worked out.

Uncommon Sense: Actually Knowing What You're Talking About

The best publicists take the time to learn about their client in sufficient detail that they can intelligently, thoughtfully pitch a reporter who covers the applicable industry or market. Someone tasked with marketing a story should, as a basic foundation, take the time to learn about who, what, where, and when to pitch a story or profile idea, and why it would benefit a particular publication and its readers. Presumably, a publicist has some specialization—consumer technology, fashion, hospitality—and knowledge about pitching those specific types of stories. The real challenge is figuring out who to pitch and what the desired goal should be.

Let's say you're a publicist covering companies in the digital-security space. You want to find a time hook that doesn't feel opportunistic. In a way, a scandal like the credit-card hacks that targeted Home Depot or Target can be a godsend for you (as terrible as it is for the victims in those cases). You have a couple of options when this sort of thing falls into your lap. You can dash off and send original pitches to TV or radio producers who book on-air talent for show hosts. You can tout the organization you represent and explain how the company CEO is an expert on the topic at hand. You then explain how the well-spoken, camera- or microphone-ready CEO you represent can succinctly explain why the current scandal is important to the program's audience.

Is there part of that suggested way to pitch that strikes you as novel? Notice I didn't mention pitching the product or what the

41

company does, aside from including a brief, relevant description about how the organization or executive relates to the matter at hand. In this situation, what you're *not* selling is the business directly. By establishing your executive as an expert on the matter, you're establishing your credibility as an expert so that the audience will associate you with the subject matter.

The same is true if you're pitching yourself as the expert, whether you're a small-business owner, an executive, or someone who just likes being an opinionated thought leader. Your aim in this scenario is to get yourself in front of the world and let people know you exist, and you must focus on providing value for the program's audience and your hosts, since they will directly and indirectly compose your network in the future. Resist the urge to do something short-sighted like talking about your product on national TV. Instead, focus on providing legitimate, helpful information to a wide audience, and you'll be able to reap the rewards down the road, in the form of continued exposure, good relationships, and a steady stream of business brought in by the best kind of referral: positive word of mouth.

Being a helpful, gracious guest, one who's there to offer a few useful sentences to tell a story, may not seem like the biggest deal in the world, but it'll lead to producers calling you back again and again. Producers and hosts are just like you: they want their jobs to be done well, with people they know and trust, in a timely, efficient manner. Make their lives easier by providing real value without any drama, and you'll gain a reputation for being smart as well as for having expertise as a businessperson and improving your company's image as you build your own.

No matter what you're pitching—whether it's a traditional business, something more intangible (like an app), or a book or film—your pitch will be most successful if you can add value to whatever medium you are pitching. The wording and tone of your pitch will vary every time, but the core message remains the same: "This [person, object, or service] will make your article better, make your TV show more entertaining and informative, or draw more readers to your website."

Now, you can't directly say that, because it may suggest that a reporter doesn't know how to do his or her job without your help. Rather, you simply want to state the facts: you or the person you are promoting knows a lot about a specific topic and has some thoughts on the subject. Potentially include some of those thoughts, and make sure they're useful (such as quotes that demonstrate specific knowledge and that could enhance a story that's already part of the news cycle). You may still fail. That's fine. We all fail more than we'd like. That doesn't mean that 10 or 100 failed pitches won't finally lead to one bit of coverage, and that one guest appearance or interview won't then lead to more.

You can and should be mercenary in trying to get coverage for whatever you need to, but you also must keep in mind the interests of the other party and how you can help them. Being mindful of how to be truly helpful is the difference between success and failure in the PR game. If you can be the man or woman who is useful to a reporter and help her do her job with more ease and flexibility, she will be much more likely to hear you out and see if you fit into what she's covering in the future. If you're good at what you're doing, you should be bringing her the type of thing that will be interesting to her and her audience. I built an entire business on snagging clients about whom I knew reporters were already writing. And this, as you might note, goes right back to what I was saying about knowing your industry and what's going on in a particular field.

Never discount that journalists are real human beings and have interests of their own. Like anyone else, they have likes and dislikes, and if they actually like what you are pitching, you will have earned at least an audience of one. If they don't write about your product or company even though they like it, it may be because they couldn't find a way to make it work. That happens more often than you'd believe. Even the best journalists can't always sell their editors on the stories they love. But if they like what you're doing, maybe they'll revisit it later. Maybe they'll just appreciate that you brought them something great.

Or maybe they'll say and do nothing, and you'll move on.

Filling the Content Void

The 24-hour news cycle may be the bane of anyone who's ever been stuck in a waiting room or airport boarding area, but in business, there's a way to use it to your advantage. Every media outlet has become an amorphous, junkie-like vacuum for content. This means reporters are required to produce more content than ever, but that often gives them license to report on new things they think are genuinely interesting and exciting. They are pitched so many horrible products by hordes of indifferent PR people that a well-formed pitch about a topic or company that would be worth covering is a breath of fresh air in their daily professional lives.

This is not, however, to say that reporters are desperate and grateful that PR people are there to fling stories at them daily. Most reporters have their jobs because they're insatiably curious people who are also pretty good, and possibly gifted, at uncovering new ideas, trends, and stories. When it comes to pitches, it can be a stunning rarity that someone actually brings a reporter something she wants and can use. When you accomplish that, chances are she might be somewhat grateful. I say *somewhat* because many reporters are, understandably, wary of not wanting to be the channel through which a PR person makes money. They don't want to shill. They want to write about things that readers want to read about. They want to provide information to the public, for the public's good. Never forget that.

The other aspect is that media—especially online media—constantly needs to be fed to in turn feed its audience, and the public relations industry has benefited enormously from this. Even if you're pitching yourself, for whatever thing you're doing in whatever medium, you can maintain this kind of cadence with reporters and benefit from it as well. Just make sure you're going after the right writers at the right publications.

Who You'll Be Pitching

Before we dive even deeper into how to pitch and how to position yourself, let's establish a basic truth: there are people who write, and people who broadcast. Within these organizational structures, there are various gatekeepers who control what goes on the website, into the print magazine, or onto the television show.

You want to work with these people.

At a basic level, you want to figure out who to approach.

Now, from there, you've got a bunch of different categories of people, and knowing *who* to talk to is both crucially important and confusing as hell, because these titles can apply to both print and broadcast. But I'll explain it all.

Bloggers: A blogger can be anybody from some guy in a stained undershirt ranting in his mom's basement to Andrew Sullivan, the first blogger to actually be paid good money by his readers on a subscription basis. These can also be people on Twitter, Instagram, or YouTube (some PR types obnoxiously call them "influencers") who have a sizable reach and might be in a good position to promote your wares.

You can generally reach bloggers with a short, tightly focused email pitch. But before you do so, make sure that you're familiar with not only who they are but who their audience is, what specific niche they appeal to, and whether they have a lot of dedicated fans they engage with. (If that's the case, maybe you want to give them some samples to give away.) Some blogs and video channels have their own inside jokes and other references that only die-hard followers will understand. Understanding these nuances will score you big points, so do your research by following along for a few weeks and understanding who you're pitching beforehand. It's also really strange to me that I have to mention this, but *actually read or watch their stuff.* I know that seems so delightfully obvious! In fact, it's not that obvious, and many PR people and individuals pitching products tend not to do that basic (if slightly time-consuming) research.

Reporters: Unlike bloggers, reporters are (sort of) a rare breed these days, but that means you'll probably find them working for bigger outlets, such as regional or national magazines or newspapers, which have more established processes. Whereas a blogger's story won't necessarily be edited, be fact-checked, or have a deadline (which can be both good and bad), a reporter's story will go through all those steps. That means you have a better shot of getting your story told accurately, though it may have a smaller audience and not be as timely. The real difference comes down to the layers of support a reporter will have (for example, copy editors at newspapers or even research departments at major magazines) and the level of reporting they'll do. The line between blogger and reporter has become increasingly blurred, however, as blogs like TechCrunch and Engadget have given some bloggers the weight of full-fledged reporters. Confusing, right? Sort of. But it doesn't have to be.

Initially, you should pitch a reporter the same way you might pitch a blogger: with a short, concise pitch that can give them something relevant to report on. You'll want to research the reporter's beat (her area of coverage, be it a specific industry, company, region, market, or area of interest) and make sure that whatever you're suggesting falls within that. You should also be sure to do your homework on what she writes but also on any specific *way* she reports. Some reporters freelance for a lot of publications and therefore cover certain angles regularly, such as diversity issues in technology. Or she might have one full-time job and write about certain kinds of cars.

One main difference between bloggers and reporters is that with reporters, there's a good chance that your relationship will last beyond one pitch if you handle the relationship respectfully and aren't a pest. Reporters need sources, and they stand a good chance of coming to you when they need something. At that point, you'll probably step up your communication from email to the phone or in-person. But for now, you want to keep it strictly electronic. *Do not call or text a reporter unannounced.* There is no better way than cold-calling to prematurely prejudice a reporter against you before you even start your pitch.

Producers: In the same way that you should never pitch a reporter by phone, you should never pitch a broadcast journalist, ever. To be specific, that person you see reading the news is 99 percent of the time not the person you want to send a product to or talk to about a product. What you're looking for is a *producer.* That's the person who produces (get it?) the show, works out the content for the show, and finds the guests for the show. While print reporters are responsible for finding their own stories, radio and TV hosts generally do not have to seek them out. Instead, they have people, known as producers, whose job it is to find stories for their programs.

There will be different ranks among the producers, such as production assistant, executive producer, and other titles. Generally, finding stories falls to the more-junior production assistants. Sometimes you can actually find a single person at a show who *literally books guests* (they're usually called "booker" or "guest booker" or something like that). This doesn't mean that they will book any guest you throw at them, but the net result is that if you can make a case that this is a unique, good-for-TV-or-radio person, they'll be more likely to take them on.

The nice thing about broadcast is that there are so many different kinds of programs that you can probably find plenty of outlets for you to pursue. A health and wellness product or service could be pitched to something like *Dr. Oz,* a radio program on NPR, or even a segment on CNBC or *Bloomberg Business*, if you can figure out the right angles. As ever, don't call producers on the phone. Email them.

Finally, there is one slight annoyance about broadcast: the chicken and the egg argument. Many producers will respond with, "Have they done TV before?" If you haven't done it before, you will have a lot of problems getting on television. A good way to avoid this is to get yourself some sort of speaking engagement that you film. The result is that you'll at least have some way to prove that you won't go on TV or radio and be totally and utterly dull.

Specialists: Specialists are a segment that you may not think about but could be immensely valuable. Think of these as reporters, writers, or producers who work for a trade magazine, for a special-interest journal, or in some kind of obscure niche programming. These types of outlets are great. One might have a small audience, but the people reading or tuning in are probably so deeply into a particular niche that it is in their interest to stay abreast of every single development in that world. There are special publications for almost every market, industry, and type of infrastructure, from pizzerias to parking ramps. Readers of these types of publications are often executives, high-level consultants, or experts in that particular field or industry and can be an important audience to reach. The flipside is that unless you have a very specific pitch that is precisely homed in on what the specialist covers, you are probably wasting that editor or producer's time.

Ideally, you will approach a specialist publication that you are already aware of, and you will be confident that they will be interested in covering you or your product. This could turn into an ongoing story and a source-type relationship similar to a reporter. This blends into the reporter and blogger angle, but occasionally very niche blogs and outlets, such as Employee Benefit News (for HR professionals) or the one-man blog that is Brian Krebs (security), might enjoy working with you and promoting what you do.

Know Who You're Pitching

Having an effective pitch is only part of the equation. You also need to know *who* you're pitching. This does not mean creating an exhaustive dossier on them in some stalker-like manner; this can be immensely creepy, as many reporters have told me horror stories of PR people faking relationship knowledge using their Instagram and Facebook feeds. What you do want to do is some pretty extensive research on what a specific reporter has written about, which outlets he has written for in the past, what he posts on social media, what's relevant on his LinkedIn profile, and any other intelligence you can gather on him. Understanding his coverage now and in the past (Google is your friend) can help you see, as a fellow human, the clear lines around what really interests him.

This is distinct from the types of topics a reporter covers, since some topics on a specific beat will naturally be more interesting to certain individuals. Just because a writer covers enterprise software doesn't mean she wouldn't rather write only about consumer gadgets. Sometimes this isn't immediately obvious, and you'll need to use your judgment and intuition to gain a better understanding of what interests which reporters.

Another great way to dig up information is Twitter feeds. Many reporters just post their own stories. Some reporters talk constantly with other reporters or their readers. Either way, you'll likely get a good handle on what kind of person a reporter is and, most importantly, how you can approach her.

Some people are ultra-formal and require a certain cerebral approach through a pitch that's a bit more formally structured. Conversely, many reporters actually love being approached on a very informal manner, something as casual as, "Here's a thing that you may like and may want to write about. Here's what it is, and here's why you should give a shit."

As you might infer, this is way more of an art than a science, and the best way to learn is, unfortunately, from your mistakes. The only vaguely stalker-ish thing to do might be to follow their tweets. Many reporters, bloggers, and *even normal people* use Twitter to talk about what they're interested in, share their thoughts on the day's issues, or just make silly jokes. This can give you insight into the type of person you're pitching and some degree of perspective on how to approach him. Every pitch should also have a degree of personality, just as any conversation with different people should. Some people might be quite cavalier and colloquial, and thus you can approach them in a way that's more silly and jokey (though you should never *try* to be funny). Some people that you observe may have a more reserved and calm personality, and you'll want to pitch them in that manner.

Once you've done the groundwork, you're ready to pitch. Remember that any reporter of note, even at tiny publications or no-name radio stations, receives at least 50 unsolicited emails from PR people a day. You're hoping that your email gets read, and if it does, you need to get in and out with the information in front of them as quickly as possible. You want to keep your pitches short—ideally fewer than 100 words, but no more than 150. Your pitch must describe whatever it is you're pitching (duh) and why it matters to the person you're pitching it to.

Classic public relations training will instruct you to "tell a reporter why it's important," but you want to go a step further and tell him why it's important *to him*. This is where your background research on the reporters comes in handy. You have to be able to tailor your pitch to the reporter based on how useful it is to what he's writing about. Not doing so is at best laziness and at worst a sign of disrespect. Either of those is a good way to get your pitch thrown into the virtual trash.

You must make a pitch appeal not only to a reporter but also to his audience. He knows his audience better than you do, no matter how much research you do, no matter how great you think you are. You are targeting him first, but more generally, you need to know the market segment he reaches.

Crafting the Pitch

Most pitches from PR pros and publicists are awful. And they're awful because they're usually more about how cool, intelligent, and insightful the publicist thinks he is, rather than about the client or the product. It might also be about how supposedly great the client is but not about *why* said client is great. This also happens when founders and random individuals pitch themselves for TV shows, touting how smart and interesting they are with *absolutely no justification as to why.*

Since, if you're pitching yourself or hiring someone to pitch on your behalf, this is your time and money on the line, and you need to be economical with your words. In doing so, you'll make things easier for whomever you're pitching.

Your objective is to deliver the most information with the fewest words. This is your first and best chance to convey key concepts and facts to your initial audience (reporters, producers, etc.). Nothing more.

Personally, I have three hard rules I stick to at all costs when I am pitching someone.

1. Keep it under 150 words. Go for 125, if you can.

2. Be direct. No jargon, no fluff.

3. Write. Do not copy and paste. That is, write each pitch individually, for each person, each time.

One caveat: If you've found a clever, pithy way of describing yourself or your product, don't remake the wheel. If you've found a way to distill something quickly and accurately, keep it. Modify it slightly, of course, for each person.

When you follow these rules, you can craft something that will not only help the reporter but also help you get better at pitching reporters and thinking about what you're trying to pitch. Rewriting the same basic pitch again and again will help you refine your understanding of your product or service and help you be a more effective communicator overall.

You're not trying to pitch a story to the reporters, either. They have plenty to write about, and a lot of it is generated in their own heads. Instead, you want to convey information that is useful to them and their readers. Just as you are providing a good or a service to your customers, you are also providing a service to the reporter by giving them high-quality material to use as content for their publication. If you're not, you fucked up your targeting.

How to Make Sure You Get Noticed

When you think about your email subject line, think about a newspaper headline. Can you write a catchy headline? If not, you better start there.

Headlines are so important that newspapers used to keep a writer on staff whose only job was to write headlines. (What a quaint notion today, that there was once an era when headlines weren't governed by search engine optimization and other algorithmic shenanigans.) Nowadays, that job is gone thanks to massive budget cuts, but the importance of headlines remains the same. Your headline must be focused and to-the-point but also interesting enough to draw your target in further. This is your one chance to get his attention, so make it count.

A general rule is that your headline should reflect as much of the pitch's information as possible. A common mistake is to assume that the *entire* pitch should be in there. What you want is for it to say what you need it to, such as "Guest Idea: Guy Who Has X Years in Cybersecurity and a Company Worth Y Millions." You want to give someone a reason to open the email. The Lily Camera's subject headline was, roughly, "Flying Robot Camera—Throw It in the Air, It Starts Flying and Follows You."

Think about misleading headlines you've seen on clickbait web stories. You don't want to waste a reporter's time by writing that way. If your email subject line doesn't reflect your pitch (or is boring), there's a good chance the recipient will feel like you were trying to mislead them or, worse, waste their time. All that means is that you've burnt a bridge before it was even built.

Some reporters have told me that writing the content first makes it easier to come up with a headline, while others swear that having the title first makes the writing easier. Personally, I prefer the latter. Either way, focusing on a headline will force you to home in on what you're really trying to convey versus trying to craft an eloquent but unnecessary five-word description.

Pitching 101

Pitching is how you get reporters to write about your client. The pitch itself is the story you want them to write.

As with novels or screenplays, there are generally a few formulas that should be used when crafting a pitch. There can be crossover amongst the archetypal pitches, but they don't usually deviate from the basic structure. Knowing them cold will make your life a lot easier.

Type 1: Company Story

"X Company Is the Y for Z." This formula is used a great deal in technology, be it for a new website or a new product. How many times have you heard that "X is the Uber/Facebook/Apple of Y"? But giving people an analogous example is one of the biggest clichés in tech publicity for a reason. People live for familiarity and schemata. Give them a reference point.

The media are always hungry for good stories on new and interesting companies, but they also get pitched on them multiple times a day, so it's essential you do everything you can to pique their interest. You may be able to get away with a story on the company itself, or your pitch may need to incorporate a unique angle like how the founder's inspiration came from some traumatic or serendipitous event or harrowing circumstances. I once pitched a client whose entire company had to be shut down, only to be brought back from the ashes using a different angle on what they did. The resulting article was huge for them personally and professionally.

Type 2: Company News

A new source of funding, a change in management, or the introduction of a new product or service can be great sources of company news. The first two can be big stories in the financial press or in specialty publications like trade journals or industry-focused blogs. Product rollouts are obviously of wider interest but might be more difficult to place in the mainstream media.

Type 3: Trend Pieces

These are a little more difficult to pitch. You'll need a big-picture view that helps tie you into a broader context. For example, say you've created an app for people who want to grow vegetables in their urban backyards. Your pitch could be tied into the growing trend of urban farming. Maybe there's a local user you could pitch to a regional publication as a feel-good profile. There's also a food element in this story, which is another big topic these days, especially local, organic, and sustainable produce, like the kind grown by your client's target audience. This works best for blogs, magazines, and other outlets that aren't big on time-sensitive hard news and focus on softer, human-interest-style feature articles.

The important thing to remember is that you don't want to force a trend. If it doesn't exist, if you don't have hard evidence that it's real, the person reading the pitch will not be a particularly big fan of yours. Good examples of bad trend stories are lists of three other companies doing similar things as your client's company, vague statistics or survey data that you didn't come up with and that doesn't actually say much (for example, "40 Percent of Americans Do X," from a sample of 40 people), and straight-up fabricated trends that you wish existed, if only to make yourself or your client look good.

Type 4: Sourcing

Sit down and read a story in the newspaper, and you'll inevitably see someone quoted—a lawyer, a doctor, a person of interest within the story who isn't necessarily part of it. For example, I introduced a reporter who was working on a story about the user interfaces of new phones to a client that makes Android apps more user-friendly. Unsurprisingly, the reporter was happy, because the client was actually useful to her. The client was happy because they got their name associated with a big story.

If you or someone you work with is an expert on a topic that is tangentially related to your product, this is a good way to get some publicity. You are effectively playing matchmaker for a reporter in this situation. As I mentioned earlier when explaining how to provide value as an expert on a television show, it's important that whoever is being interviewed provides a direct answer to the reporter's questions and does not use the interview as an opportunity to plug the business or themselves. The payoff here comes from being seen as an expert or thought leader.

It's also a good way to, as I've repeatedly said, make friends with a reporter, producer, or blogger. Every writer reporting on a topic wants to have sources to make their story more than an opinion piece. If you're a *good* source and not just someone waffling about yourself, you'll have helped a reporter do less legwork, saving her valuable time and helping her be more efficient.

How to Follow Up

Even when you email a reporter a really specific pitch, she may not respond. Don't harass her. Give her a few days between replies—follow up once, maybe twice. But no more. If she's not getting back to you after two follow-ups, it's a lost cause. You want to hound her only if she's shown interest in your work and then suddenly gone dark. If she's never responded, well, that's just how it goes. You're not going to win them all.

In the rare scenario where someone shows interest and suddenly goes quiet, it's OK to email her one or two more times, or perhaps (if she follows you) direct message her on Twitter. However, just as with a normal pitch, if she disappears and doesn't circle back, assume she's no longer interested. Sorry, she doesn't work for you.

As you get more experience pitching, your pitches will get better, and you'll learn from your mistakes. It's an iterative process and unfortunately one that can't be learned overnight. But if you're not harassing reporters, then at the very least, you'll make and maintain some media contacts, rather than burning your bridges right at the outset.

Pitching Someone by Phone

Emails can be annoying, but an unscheduled phone call is invasive and always a bad idea. I strongly advise you to avoid calling reporters or producers.

But—and this is a big "but"—some people don't want to be pitched over email. They just think it's another form of spam, no matter how sincere you might be. It will happen only every so often, but you'll have to be ready to engage these types over the phone when it does. They are likely old-school journalists who would rather be writing on a Smith Corona than on a MacBook.

Before you dial, have a 30- to 60-second pitch ready to go. Relax. Do *not* script what you plan to say. Get an idea of what you want to convey and how you want to say it. If you're struggling, jot down bullet points but nothing more. If you can, avoid "umms," "aahs," and any filler words.

Imagine before you call that you are talking to, as you most likely are, someone with very little time who is not interested in what you have to say. Speak like a normal person, and get your point across quickly. Lead by saying, "Do you have about a minute to chat?" (You can even say that you mean "a minute" literally.) I also like, "Is this a good time?"

If they say "No," say, "Sorry" and that you'll call them back. If they sound not-annoyed to hear from you, ask when you can call them. If they sound annoyed, say, "Sorry," and never call them again.

If they say anything about being on deadline, get off the phone as quickly as possible and be very apologetic. Do not ask them anything. Don't hang up, but basically do as little talking as possible, and let them get on with work.

It's better to be polite and respectful than risk burning that bridge forever (and if they are older, manners probably mean more to them than you expect). Remember, you can always call back another time.

If they say to go on, the pitch should include three details. Tell the reporter who you are, why you're calling, and what exact, interesting topic or trend is worth reporting. You should also be easy to understand and make sense to the person you're calling. As a courtesy to the reporter, make sure you know his name and pronounce it correctly. As someone with an obscure last name (Zih-tron, not Zay-tron, Zie-tron, Zoo-tron, or anything else), I know that having my name pronounced incorrectly is an excellent way to sour my mood. Yes, that sounds like I'm a jerk (I am), but if you're already calling someone to bother him about something for your benefit, mispronouncing his name makes you sound rude.

Though I don't think any decent reporter will argue with you about the substance of your pitch or the nature of your client's business when you're on the phone pitching them, it never hurts to be ready for your own on-the-spot interview.

Some of the common questions you might be asked:

▶ Why is this better than X?

▶ <Insert difficult technical question>

▶ Why are you calling me?

It can help to prepare your answers to these questions ahead of time. There are two ways to think about this.

One, you can answer the questions as honestly as possible. This also means as quickly and directly as possible. No buzzwords, no filler, no nonsense. Don't lie, don't dodge questions (unless you think the person is messing with you), and be ready to give them real-life information.

If you're a PR person, never reply, "Oh, well, I can't answer that, but do you want to talk to the CEO?" That is a complete waste of everyone's time, and reporters hate it. Frankly, a lot of executives hate it, too. They hired you. Do your job.

Or two, you can answer the questions with more questions. This is generally a risk but one that you can mitigate by making sure your questions are good ones—better ones, in fact. This is not a move for amateurs. Veteran reporters have heard it all and are used to getting fluffy, evasive answers from PR people and interview subjects. They might test you with questions just to mess with your head, or they might really be trying to see what you're made of. On the other hand, honesty always builds respect between two people. Keep the conversation light and easy, and don't spend too much time trying to convince someone who seems angry or overly critical.

Salvaging a Bad Phone Call

When you start to get the feeling that your phone call isn't going as well as you planned, you will be tempted to hang up and pretend your cell provider dropped the call. I've done it. Before you do so, make sure it's not salvageable. If the person clearly hates you and is just pissed off that you called, get off the phone as quickly as possible and try, if you can, not to cry too much in the nearest bathroom stall.

However, if they're simply *argumentative* and disagreeing with you, you need to double down and approach the phone call like a professional.

First things first—keep a cool head. I know, I know, that's easier said than done. On an instinctual level, it's easy to react badly to adversity. As someone with what could be described as terminal anxiety, I am all too familiar with the blurry vision, sweaty palms, and general unease that can happen when someone is unexpectedly tearing you a new one.

The problem is that you can find yourself matching their tone of voice and their energy (that is, yelling right back at them and losing your shit) even if you don't intend to. This will not help you at all. Instead, lower your voice. Take a deep breath to slow your breathing. It's cliché, I know, but it really does work, so do it. Feel your heart rate slow down, and let the color come back into your face. Are you calm and collected now? Good.

You can regain your footing by asking him why he is upset. This is a very subtle, unthreatening way of calling out someone on uncouth behavior. If he is a decent, rational person, he will usually back down and explain his frustration or even apologize.

If the person on the other end of the line keeps screaming at you and making a fuss, then thank him for his time, and hang up. It doesn't matter who he is. It's not worth trying to deal with him. (Also, I'd go so far as to say people screaming at you on the phone are, in general, not worth trying to please or work with.)

A Note About Pitching TV

I'll be honest with you, dear reader. Pitching TV guests is *hard*. I know one TV producer who gets 1000 emails a day. (No, I'm not exaggerating. She is a producer on a well-known news program that you probably watch.) And 99.9 percent of the pitches that hit her inbox get lost in the ether. I heard anecdotally that a producer for Jon Stewart's *The Daily Show* received more than *10,000* emails a day.

To get on TV, you have to jump through hoops before you'll even be considered. If you're not in a major media hub (New York, Los Angeles, and, to a lesser extent, Washington, D.C.), you need to be close to a studio in a major metro area. And then you need to be available at the exact time that the TV producer has open for you. If that's on the West Coast, then yes, you will be required to be in the chair, with makeup done, at 5 a.m. so that you can be on the 8 a.m. timeslot on the East Coast. It is not fun. If you can't make it on time or be at the studio, forget it. There are 999 other people who would kill their own mother to get on the air. It doesn't even necessarily have to be the biggest television show; there's a mystique around being on TV that means that people will fight tooth and nail to land a spot.

Of course, that's assuming you have even made it that far. The best way to get an introduction to a TV producer is in person, or at least via a very warm, kind introduction from a friend or colleague. You'll need to network like hell to even get an introduction. That will vault you past other candidates who are just trying to get a chance to pitch the producer. They're usually, in my experience, very nice, just immensely overwhelmed with terrible emails and a very hard job. If you can help them have an easier life, they will appreciate you very, very much.

Television also has very specific requirements for a guest, far beyond being available at a moment's notice. TV producers likely already have a solid Rolodex of contacts they can call upon for an expert opinion. These are high-level individuals who are generally established names in their field. They typically have data and years of expertise to back up their opinions and are adept at getting their point across in very short bursts, punctuated by questions that vary in intensity and difficulty. That's not to say that you or someone within your organization lacks experience or competence for this sort of media appearance. It's just that the bar to get a TV appearance is quite high, and it only gets higher and higher and doesn't let up, even when you're sitting in the chair, waiting to do a live take.

Pitching, Hacking, and How to Be Seen on TV

I mentioned digital security and getting on TV earlier for a reason: getting a digital-security client on TV has consistently been one of the biggest challenges in my career. Getting on TV is hard. Getting a security-related client on TV is harder because there are so many talking heads available. Many of them are, quite frankly, worthless and offer nothing unique or of substance. But they offer something to time-crunched, stressed-out producers: the ready availability of a figure who is accepted as an authority and can quickly be rallied during a major security crisis.

I've even had reporters complain to me that said figures are useless beyond pushing the "Security is good!" mantra. But in the midst of a major scandal (think Heartbleed or another major security breach that puts millions of consumers or computer users at risk for financial loss), they can be counted upon to give at least one good sound bite on short notice. And that's often enough for a producer, even if my client would be better suited for their program.

It gets even harder if your product or service is pretty similar to the rest of the pack. If you are truly unremarkable and have no differentiating features, then it will be that much harder to get yourself noticed. The best advice I have for you is to make a better product. Harsh, I know, but a better use of your time than continuously hitting people up to feature your product.

A better product in this case doesn't even have to mean the best product. It's about utility. It's about a differentiator between you and the rest of the known universe. It may be that although you're yet another security expert, you're also incredibly interesting and good at TV. You may have a messaging application that also has a particularly weird feature—like a client of mine that offers the ability to send messages along with Bitcoin transfers.

The same was true for me as I tried to set myself apart as a publicist. It took a long time before people took me seriously as a PR person, because apart from being British, I seemed to offer very little else that was different.

What eventually set me apart were several things:

- I was willing to actively talk about an industry's negative sides, which many people were quite content to ignore.

- I was very quotable, I was almost always available for comment, and I'd read up on every subject to an obsessive level.

- I'm weird. This may not seem like much, but when you're a bit weird and different (there's that word again) from the other however-many-hundred people, it helps.

- I would say things that weren't generic or obvious.

What to Do When They Start Coming to You

At some point, people will start coming to you to get the scoop on what you're doing. Sometimes you can't give it to them. Maybe you're not ready to talk about what's in the works, like a new feature or product rollout. If that's the case, being honest is best. This may mean you say, "I really can't talk about that right now." Or if you need to not even acknowledge that something is in the works, you can say, "I don't know what you're talking about," listen carefully to the questions being asked, and reply, "Huh, I'll look into that."

The moment you lie or withhold, you start to lose the confidence of those around you—your colleagues, your network, and the media contacts that you've worked so hard to cultivate. If you can't say what you're working on or you can't give a reporter what he's looking for (at least not yet), just promise that you'll get him everything when you have it. That's all you can (or should) do. The last thing you want to do is give out incomplete information that might be confusing. Your intention, of course, is not to confuse anyone, but when that happens, it often comes across not as partial information but as outright dishonesty. So be on the safe side. This may mean you eventually let down or annoy a reporter. It's better to do that than lie or give crappy information. This will almost always lead to exactly one result: a much angrier reporter.

For those reporters who always tell the right story (that is, the one that helps you out), it's important to reward them. Sure, that's their job—to be accurate and to report on what's going on in the world—and they don't necessarily deserve a gold star and a ribbon just for doing their job. But that's not the world we live in. But in fairness to

65

the media, with the speed of reporting on the web and budget cuts loading more work on reporters' desks, it's easier than ever to do a bad job. So it's important to recognize reporters who make the effort to do their jobs well and give them some special attention.

There are a couple of ways to do that. Offer a reporter you like the first glimpse at new products. Invite her to the office, and show her around. Better yet—because she's probably short on time—take her to lunch or buy her a drink and introduce her to other important people in your organization or network. Give her behind-the-scenes details of upcoming events. Give her everything you can, and more often than not, she'll give you everything she can. Make a little extra effort to show her substantive, informational angles that others haven't seen, and make sure she knows about things first—a reward that is, ultimately, more access for working with you.

The more you monitor the media to see how various reporters treat your client, the better you'll know who to reward and who to avoid. There is no rule that says you have to pursue an equal number of reporters who are sympathetic and unsympathetic to your client. Those who are unsympathetic or are not treating you or your client well are not worth your time. You are better off finding other people with whom to share your ideas and stories. Those are the people—the ones who produce the kind of coverage that is fair and, ideally, positive—who should get the best stuff.

building your brand, creating content, and not sucking at both

Countless studies (http://werbepsychologie-uamr.de/files/ literatur/01_Iyengar_Lepper(2000)_Choice-Overload.pdf, http://www.apa.org/monitor/jun04/toomany.aspx, http://www-2.rotman .utoronto.ca/bicpapers/pdf/04-08.pdf) have shown that having too much choice can end up resulting in inaction. However, a great deal of people who want to sell something think that the best possible course of action is to be everywhere, all the time. I remember, when I moved to the US from the UK, being amazed at how many different kinds of yogurt were available in the supermarket. What would have taken up a small shelf at a grocery store at home was nearly an entire aisle. I was overwhelmed by the sheer number of choices and ended up just grabbing the first container I saw and walking away. It was strawberry, and the awful kind with the bits in it. Sadly, when I got home to the UK, I found that the same thing had happened to the yogurt aisle there. The world's getting worse, one yogurt at a time.

You may, at times, feel the same way about social media, blog posts, and other stuff that PR types would call content creation. As with yogurt, soda, cereal, and almost everything in a supermarket, most of it isn't worth eating. It's loaded with unhealthy crap, it tastes bad, or it expires really quickly. But some of it is delicious and worthwhile. The sad and strange part of social media, though, is that if the Internet were a supermarket, you'd find the yogurt company also trying to make athletic equipment, portable music players, hats, and cat food because people seem to like those things.

That sounds ridiculous. Except most brands desperately create a Twitter account, a Facebook page, a YouTube channel, and even a Pinterest board. These are brands that have no reason to bother with any of this.

Why, for example, does Clorox need a Pinterest page? I'm not particularly sure. A Twitter account might make sense to answer questions or offer gentle reminders like, "Please do not drink Clorox." But the manufacturing giant has a Pinterest account (http://www .pinterest.com/Clorox), which proudly declares, "We laugh in the face of mess. And we've got the pins to prove it." At the time of this writing, it has a whopping 559 followers. That's a full 20,000 fewer than I have on Twitter, and while I might leave a bad taste in your mouth, I am by no means the most popular form of bleach.

This may seem a tad befuddling, so I'm going to give you a quick (well, as quick as possible) and dirty guide to social media, blogs, press releases, and other forms of content that you can use to spread your message. More importantly, I'll also make sure you understand why you do or do not want them.

Before You Even Sign Up For A Social Media Account, Read This

Whether you are handling PR for yourself or for someone else, your biggest time suck should be pitching or networking.

I can say with confidence that, if you go down the wrong path, you'll spend far more time managing various social media accounts, be it Facebook, Twitter, YouTube, or your company blog, and it will take up a silly number of hours. A good pitch, on the other hand, will take you 5 to 10 minutes, tops.

It's very easy to get sucked in to signing up for and setting up all kinds of social media nonsense. To avoid this, it helps to take stock of what your goals are and what you're hoping to accomplish with not just your social accounts but your larger public relations strategy. There's a sexy temptation to having a so-called presence online, as if not having one will somehow make people say or think that you don't exist. However, this is true if you have a website and nothing else, so I'd recommend at least one kind of social media account. Knowing how to interact on various platforms can have its functional uses, but with so many options and so many so-called success stories of companies with multiple accounts, you may think you can copy your way to success. Look at the disparity between the accounts maintained by file-sharing service Box and the company's CEO, Aaron Levie. One is straight corporate data, and the other—which is quite beloved—reads like the Silicon Valley equivalent of comedian Jerry Seinfeld (but so much worse). Levie has clearly mastered the medium, whereas his company's accounts are nothing less than lackluster.

You might be asking yourself: so how do I even get started? Let's start small.

Below is a questionnaire I give to new clients when I want to make them understand the point of hiring me. I want you to fill it out for yourself, but this time I've added some prompts for you to think about. If you really want to send it to me, email it to ed@ezpr.com. The exercise is about not just making the client answer the questions but also having them rethink any weird reasoning they may have behind things they do or want to pay me to do on their behalf.

You can use the answers to help inform your overall PR strategy. You might also realize how to do something better or that you want to stop doing something entirely.

- Why do you need public relations services?

- What PR tools have you used in the past?

- What does your company do, and why does it matter?

- How is your reputation working for you?

- How is your reputation not working for you?

- Where do you want to be seen or written about?

- What are your current PR needs?

- What do you want to see as a result of hiring a publicist?

- What marketing tools do you already use?

- How is the company seen in your market?

- What will make you happy with our relationship?

- What are your goals?

- What is your current PR strategy?

- What have you already done to promote yourself?

- What other publicists or firms have you worked with?

- How did that work well for you?

- What didn't work well for you?

- Who is your audience?

- Who is your target audience?

- Do you have a brand?

- How would you characterize your brand?

- What do you feel you bring to your market?

- What services do you offer?

- How do you feel you can improve your services?

- What do you do that no one else can do?

- What is your story?

- How have you succeeded?

- What mistakes have been made?

- Do you think you are connecting with your audience?

- Who are your competitors?

- Do you think you're better than them? If so, why? Please answer in a minimum of a paragraph.

Obviously, if you are starting from square one, then some of these questions will be impossible to answer. But I hope that others will provide you with some insight into how you can tell the world about whatever it is that you do. If you have an amazing story about how something was created, then perhaps that should be front and center when pitching people. If you can't think of some unique selling point, then maybe you need to rethink your business altogether.

I also hope that some of these questions may change the way you're thinking about yourself, your product, or whatever it is you're doing with your life. They're engineered—as writing things down tends to be—to make you put your thoughts together in a sentence, which at times may make you say, "Now that I've written that out, it sounds rather stupid."

There are also some clients that I put through a much simpler messaging process. The reason is simple: your best messaging always comes from within. If I begin by asking you the most evocative questions—and then help you understand why certain answers need more clarity, explanation, or a grammatical correction—you'll learn how to better handle this on your own. You'll also understand why I'm conducting this sort of exercise versus simply following a paint-by-numbers PR strategy. This can lead to arguments, but it also leads clients to feel involved in and committed to the strategy.

For most clients, I ask a series of questions and usually have one that they answer in great detail, with the rest becoming auxiliary questions that we can expand as needed.

In one sentence, three sentences, one paragraph, and three paragraphs, describe one of the following:

- What your product does

- Why your product matters

- Who your product is for

- Who you are

- Why you made the product

In the case of a person who was his or her own brand, I'd use a slightly different tactic:

In one sentence, three sentences, one paragraph, and three paragraphs, please describe one of the following:

- Who you are

- Why you matter to the world at large

- What your expertise is

- Why someone should care about you more than about one of your peers

The answers can sometimes be insufferable, but the process is there to make clients, in words, spell out their thoughts. This may be an uncomfortable process because written words are more permanent than speech, but it is necessary. While nobody is 100 percent on message all the time, I recommend that whoever fills out the questionnaire have at least *some* idea of what they feel or why they do whatever they do.

Defining a Brand

I try to avoid using the word "brand" as much as possible, but I use it a lot in the next section. Like it or not, having a strong brand is extremely important. So many businesses are little more than commodities, and branding is what sets many of them apart.

Social media and other content mediums (forgive me for using such a phrase) are some of the best areas in which to show off what your brand is all about.

As far as I'm concerned, you either have a great brand, or you have nothing at all, since no brand at all is honestly better than having an uncool one.

I'll start with one very, very common situation: the outdated, tired brand that wants to rebrand. Brands that go out of style typically do so through hubris. Company executives assume that they know what they're doing without actually consulting anyone with real know-how. In the case of social media, this is usually because they hire a social media "genius" who hooks onto supposed trends, which makes a brand begin to do things in a certain way because they desperately, desperately want to be cool. It's sort of like having a visual imagery board for a bleach brand. The folks in charge of these types of conglomerates believe they are smart enough not only to do the right thing with social media marketing but to find the right person to do it *based purely on a résumé.*

Let's just make one thing clear: *a lot of people out there claim to have done branding work for PepsiCo and other well-known brands and major corporations.* But experience working with a company is not evidence that the supposed expert advice and strategizing has been a success. The way to judge a successfully rebranded entity is through a somewhat amorphous blob of searching social media, observing sales, and judging the media's reaction to the company or brand.

My natural example is Dell, a computer company that, five years ago, was known primarily for making computers that were inexpensive and equally cheap in that they routinely malfunctioned or fell apart. In the past few years, Dell has made a push toward creating products that are competitive and good, based not on what a brand marketer or CEO would think, but on what people who use laptops all the time think. I do not know what the playbook looked like, but Dell began working to create higher-quality ultrabooks (thinner, lighter, longer-battery-life laptops) and high-quality, iMac-style desktops, as well as accessibly priced monitors. The fine folks at Dell did everything they could to prove on an engineering level (versus a marketing level) that they were capable of producing higher-quality wares. The company's poor reputation was a direct result of a sub-par product, which its executives and engineers improved.

On a personal level, it's very difficult to recover from being uncool, but people can be forgiving if your worst transgression was being a bit of a bore. I've suggested before that the best way to become interesting is to read more, understand more, and speak conversationally. If you've been known as a stodgy person, the best process is *not* to go whole-hog and wear pink socks and an entire rabbit on your head but to adopt a more subtle approach.

Perhaps, on a very small level, you get drinks with a bunch of reporters (if they'll go) and just talk to them about anything but work. Perhaps it's about having a Twitter account where you talk normally, colloquially, and casually about your life. Perhaps it's making fun of yourself there. Personas are hard to alter, but over time they can be taken out of a particular perception—not very cool, sort of boring, maybe aggressively awful in some key way—and into the realm of approachable. Think of a company the same way you think about an individual. Approachable and interesting can't be faked, but they can be learned.

If your company is completely pivoting, as startups tend to, into something totally different, you potentially have a large degree of cynicism coming your way. The way out of that is to have an honest answer, not one that's full of marketing slang. Explain how and why this is happening. Admit that your past idea wasn't the best one, and why the new one will be better. Why it will help more people. Why it will make even a small part of the world better. If you're capable of articulating this in a way that doesn't make you come off like an idiot, a liar, or a swindler, you're on the right track. Again, the best possible way of succeeding in pivoting is by actually pivoting into something better. Marketing and publicity can't stop something bad from being bad.

If you're pivoting, you need to find the best people to weigh in on how your service will improve their lives. I'm not talking about a focus group. I'm talking about the sort of people in your target market who can tell you what would make them like you again. It may be a friend's kid. In the case of Dell, it may be a college student who is looking to spend $300 to $600 on a college laptop that'll withstand a few years of basic, mostly school-related use: writing papers, online research, probably a lot of illegal downloading. If you sell motorhomes, you probably need to find some burnouts or retirees.

Assuming you are starting from scratch, let's go over what you need to do to start building a brand.

Initially, all that you'll be able to do is address the tangible elements of your brand. And that's all you really need for now. A big part of your brand, as it relates to your online presence, will be about the visual and component elements. What does it (or he or she) look like? What does it do? Who is it for? Why does it exist? Really, though, your visual presence is incredibly important.

Think about Facebook for a second. The social media service has been around for more than a decade and has altered its appearance countless times. But a few elements have stayed constant. The logo, the stylized *F*, had not changed until the dramatic font change in the logo in July 2015, which most people didn't notice. What else hasn't changed? That ugly shade of blue used for the header at the top of every profile. The typography has been altered subtly over the years but remains largely as it was in the beginning. The overall effect is a consistent look and feel that could be associated only with Facebook. Consider these the tangible elements of a brand. Furthermore, the service has dramatically changed how users receive and filter information, but to an extent the site has always served one basic purpose: writing a status update in a text box and posting it for all to see.

Now, think about Facebook on a conceptual level. How do you feel about Facebook? Is it a useful service? Or is it too intrusive and creepy? Do you wish the privacy policies were easier to understand? Do you personally think Mark Zuckerberg seems like a nice, misunderstood genius? Are you impressed by his philanthropy? These are the intangible elements that are crucial to the success of the Facebook brand and that are also, to a great degree, beyond Zuckerberg's and the company's control.

The same is true for your brand. As your company grows, you might end up altering your product based on what you learn as a person or professional. Or what if, for example, you're a musician? As your musical abilities and interests evolve, you'll likely gain experiences and perspective that'll feed directly into your music and possibly alter your sound or style. It's also likely that if your popularity grows, so will the number of detractors with which you have to contend. You will consistently have to monitor how your brand and product are performing and, depending on who you are and what your product is, make decisions based on what you want and on what your customers and audience want.

As early as possible, you want to settle on the tangible aspects of creating and building your brand. If nobody on your existing team has the requisite skills—and perhaps even if they do but you could benefit from outside perspective—you should hire a graphic designer that can help you come up with an interesting logo and eye-catching color palette. Talented graphic designers have an eye and instinct for creating a unified look and feel that will serve as the visual element for your brand.

Remember that having nothing at all is better than having something mediocre. The costs of re-branding later on—in terms of both time and money—are far too high for you to bear. This may seem as if it's stepping out of the world of publicity, but publicity, the moment it steps beyond emails, can end up being almost totally visual. If something looks and feels unprofessional, even little changes can hurt it.

Here are some examples of specific brand-related choices I've made. I paid an ungodly sum to purchase the domain ezpr.com, removing the hyphen from the ez-pr.com domain I used to use for my business. To give potential and existing clients as well reporters an impression about the serious level of service I provide, I hired professional branding, coding, and design agency Electro Polymath. It's the same agency that handled branding for well-respected companies and events such as StubHub and the PGA Tour. I splurged on a high-priced agency to handle my brand because I'd been told repeatedly that even though I was providing superior services compared to other firms, my website made my agency look unserious and amateur.

What I'm getting at is something you probably already know: perception matters. And a bad image and a poor perception of your professionalism can sabotage a client relationship before it even begins.

From this point on, you'll be dealing with the intangibles of your brand, which requires a good deal of abstract thinking. The best brands in the world are remarkably consistent in deciding what they want to be associated with and what doesn't fit their brand. If your business is providing software-as-a-service solutions to municipal governments in the Midwest, then your brand will probably not feature an edgy logo, and you *definitely* don't want to post #ThrowbackThursday videos of old 2Pac songs on your Facebook page. Aside from being a horrible exercise in judgment, it would not be consistent with the message that you're sending with your brand—in this case, something useful as well as relatively conservative and business oriented. If your brand is something edgier, like a sneaker store or record label, then doing something like that is probably OK. Answering those questionnaires I showed you and defining *what* your brand is and does is the first line of defense against committing gaffes like that.

For example, for reasons I can't fathom (maybe someone on the internal marketing team wants to seem cool), the detergent brand Tide consistently sends out promoted tweets that relate to Internet trends. These can be anything from the insipid argument in 2015 about the color of a dress to the third season of the Netflix series *House of Cards*. Neither of these has anything to do with detergents. Yes, you may wash a dress with detergent. Yes, Frank Underwood, the main character in *House of Cards*, "plays dirty." Those are not connections that naturally lead the human brain to think of Tide detergent. In fact, trying to latch onto that sort of news hook or trend may actually make people (me, probably many others) think, "Wow, what a bizarre, desperate brand. Why would they tweet that? That's embarrassing."

This is actually very common during major events or news cycles. During Oscars season, every brand, including one brand of hummus, posts catchy, thought-provoking slogans such as, "Who looks best on the red carpet? Maybe it's our New Hot Hummus." I can say with complete confidence that nobody reads something stupid like that and says, "Wow, I sure do want some hummus because it is now connected to the Academy Awards, which interest me a great deal."

This desperation to be relevant can lead brands into trouble. Several brands connected to barbecue ribs, including Chili's, hooked onto the third season of *House of Cards* as an opportunity to be relevant. Or so someone incorrectly thought. It is well known to fans of the show that Frank Underwood eats ribs. The problem? Many brands that chose to advertise clearly didn't have anyone on staff actually watching the show. In the second season of *House of Cards* (and please forgive this spoiler), Frank Underwood's involvement with ribs, bought and eaten at Freddy's BBQ Joint, helps the humble restaurant's popularity spike. However, as the second season progressed, Freddy was forced to shutter the Joint and the pitmaster-chef's life was effectively ruined.

In essence, anyone who has seen the first two seasons of the show—the target audience for this particular tie-in—and sees a third season-related rib joke from a brand will think, "This brand is not just irrelevant; it is actually disconnected from popular culture."

It's also possible to straddle both sides of the cool-uncool line. Let's consider the example of Louis Vuitton. For the first 150 years of its existence, the French company made very expensive luggage and handbags for wealthy older people. But sometime around the turn of the millennium, Louis Vuitton became cool. The handbags, with the distinctive brown logo print, became a huge status symbol for younger women. The brand's commercial appeal grew around their flashy bags, and the company saw huge growth as China's luxury consumer market spiked. As sales grew, so did a new challenge: how to appeal to as many people as possible without becoming a brand associated with mass-market consumption rather than highbrow luxury.

The approach they took was fairly shrewd. The company didn't pivot toward the newer, younger, more-urban buyer. Instead, it raised prices and rigidly maintained its traditional look, even as the brand expanded into new products like men's shoes, computer bags, and clothing. This isn't to say Louis Vuitton is ignoring the newer segment of buyers; they sell smaller items, such as key pouches, belts, and wallets, that are still within reach of the lower end of luxury consumers. Brighter colors and more imaginative patterns have become part of the line, too. These moves are subtle nods to Louis Vuitton's new customers, but at the same time, the brand has managed to stick to its guns and retain a measure of authenticity, which has helped it remain popular in a very fickle marketplace.

What Louis Vuitton pulled off is advanced brand marketing. It also helps that it is part of a massive luxury-goods conglomerate staffed with marketing, public relations, and branding professionals who can devote their considerable resources to navigating these kinds of situations. But that doesn't mean you can't establish your initial brand and that, if the time comes, you can't widen its appeal while retaining your current audience.

The Biggest Secret for Social Media Success

If you can just do this one thing, you will succeed with social media. It's so simple yet so overlooked, and I can't figure out why.

Ready for it?

Ok, here it is.

Talk to people on social media.

Seriously, that's it.

Social media is a two-way conversation between you and your fans. The vast majority of brands and fan pages forget this. They use their accounts like a megaphone to blast shitty, canned messages, slogans, and URLs, without ever taking the time to engage with the people who are buying their products and willing to be advocates for the brand. This is the kind of authentic enthusiasm that companies spend billions trying to generate via advertising, marketing, and PR. When they get it for free, they don't bother.

One of my favorite examples is actor Terry Crews. As much as someone with 481,000 followers (as of this writing) can, he regularly engages with random fans. People *love* Terry Crews already. And then he, on his own and on top of being a terrific actor, makes some random person in wherever-they-are USA feel like they're special.

That's bloody *amazing*.

The best part is that it really doesn't take a long time. Even 30 minutes spent replying to Facebook posts or tweets can pay huge dividends when it comes to keeping your fans and customer base happy. In fact, even a few minutes a day can be quite powerful. Tesla CEO Elon Musk, who runs a public company and created one of the most sought-after vehicles of all time, semi-regularly responds to *random people* on Twitter. His tweets are, at times, totally scientific and utterly incomprehensible. He answers real questions (though not every question, as there are actual Tesla support channels for that), and he makes comments on things he's read.

A decade ago, social media was not what it is today, as caring about how you looked on a message board meant dealing with an audience of a few hundred people at most. Most social networks did not exist, and being a social media guru was not a real job title. The most advanced form of social media we had was Myspace, which was the LaserDisc of social sites in that it seemed really advanced at the time, but now we know it was just a lame stopgap before things really got going. It was also mostly, with performers and bands being a slight aberration, used by people to be friends with (or enemies with) people they actually knew.

When I wrote my last book, *This Is How You Pitch*, Facebook, Twitter, Instagram, and YouTube were the big players in the social media space. Since then, many more have cropped up, such as Pinterest, Snapchat, Ello, and Vine. PR professionals (as well as non-publicists) need to have a handle on most of these channels, but realistically, you'll be able to do only one or two of them really, really well, which is much better than trying to do all of them in a half-assed manner.

Before we break down the different platforms, we need to talk about the most important thing for doing social media right.

You need to keep in mind that having lots of followers on a particular network doesn't necessarily mean you're making good use of your social media accounts. If you had a shit time in high school, you might think that having 10,000 followers is pretty cool. Too bad that most of them could be "bots," otherwise known as robot spam accounts. And if you're not actually talking to the real humans following you, that's equally worthless.

Instead, the key is to find the right audience for your brand. Find the right people and have a meaningful conversation with them instead of just bombarding them with marketing messages.

Finding the right audience means knowing your client and finding people and publications that already overlap with what your client does or who your client is. A good rule of thumb is to read what reporters read, as well as what they write, about a particular topic. If you're representing a camera manufacturer, you should probably be reading DPReview, a digital photography review website. If you're interested in meta-analysis of the media, you might want to read journalist Jim

Romenesko's eponymous blog or follow *Fortune*'s Mathew Ingram on Twitter, as he often tweets about media news and technology topics. Want to dive deeper? Follow what Ingram retweets or follows. Look up the writers for DPReview. Pretty soon, you'll have a handy list of experts feeding the news you want directly into your news stream.

Social media users already hate that commercials and ads over which they have no control pop up in their feeds. Imagine how they will feel when a friend (aka your account) yammers on with annoying, pre-fab marketing speak and the same stale posts over and over again.

Think about how you can create authentic connections. I know "authentic connections" sounds like the worst corporate buzzword bullshit, but it's the best way to describe how you should focus on social media. You won't become everyone's best friend, but you do need to engage with others enough so that they start to believe there's a human being on the other end, one who is listening and actually responding to what they have to say. Offer them something of value. Tell them a good story. Make their life better. Then, maybe, they'll trust you. And when they do, when they trust you, then you can talk about things that are important to your business.

The trust you build will be what sells your business or brand. Accordingly, you shouldn't necessarily try to get people to buy what you're selling when you're on Facebook, Twitter, or Instagram. Instead, you should entertain them enough that when you do have something to sell, they're ready with their wallets. And even if you do have something to sell, you have to make them want it on their own, not through hammering them on the head with messages to buy your shit.

T-Mobile CEO John Legere turned around his fumbling, disliked carrier through a series of business moves. Some of these involved branding it as an "un-carrier," suspending the usual model of termination fees and long-term contracts. An interesting, specifically Twitter-based method he made was to harness his social media power. What that means in non-jargony human terms is that he *started posting his actual thoughts, responding to actual people, and retweeting things he actually thought were interesting.* This included attacking his competitors (including Sprint), arguing with reporters, chatting with random customers, and generally being what appears to be a quite weird and funny person. I'd guess he comes across this way because that's who he really is. The consensus among the business and technology reporters I know is that T-Mobile is no longer the carrier that you naturally equate to something you'd find inside a toilet bowl. They also seem to agree that John Legere is a great CEO who's worth listening to.

There's a rather sad, secondary lesson here, too, which is that Legere has also managed to obliterate a great deal of the good will he'd earned, by being *too* responsive and coming across as out of touch. In early 2016, he had to defend his controversial "Binge On" strategy, a T-Mobile offering in which certain (consenting) video providers' content does not count against users' data plan. There was a dark side to this: T-Mobile had throttled the quality of *all* video delivered wirelessly to smartphones, whether or not creators or specific video hosting services had agreed to be part of the program, most notably YouTube. This didn't seem fair. Surely those who *did* consent shouldn't suffer?

When the Electronic Frontier Foundation (EFF), a well-respected nonprofit dedicated to civil liberties in the digital age, questioned Legere, he responded colorfully in a shaky-cam video in which he attempted to explain his proprietary technology. He ended by asking: *Who the fuck are you, anyway, EFF? Why are you stirring up so much trouble, and who pays you?* (http://arstechnica.com/business/2016/01/john-legere-asks-eff-who-the-fk-are-you-and-who-pays-you/)

The tech community erupted. Reporters who'd applauded Legere's blunt honesty suddenly turned on him. His honest, personal Twitter presence was largely ignored because he'd not done a simple web search, let alone known a powerful industry-lobbying group by name or reputation. His thoughtless remarks led to a four-day-late mea culpa (http://www.forbes.com/sites/shelbycarpenter/2016/01/11/john-legere-apologizes-to-eff-for-dropping-f-bomb/#2715e4857a0b1c0051d3250c) that, while it placated the EFF, will never quite be forgotten as an awful, avoidable mistake.

The Second Most Important Rule: *Never Automate Your Social Media*

It's possible that you're reading this book because you're doing your own PR work in addition to your full-time duties, and that makes you an extraordinarily busy person. As such, you're the prime target for a whole host of automation tools for your social media posts. On the whole, I strongly advise you to avoid doing this at all costs. Yes, there are ways to automate your posts. Yes, you can time things and set them up to keep going at all hours of the day and night. Yes, it is that simple. And often free. But it is stupid. I can't emphasize enough how many mistakes have been made through automation, and I'll elaborate on them later.

The few times automation makes sense have to do with announcements, such as a particular product launch or a timed competition in which you're offering rewards at a certain hour or within in a specified time. Otherwise, automated posts range from weird to potentially dangerous.

First of all, does anyone think that you're online all the time? No. People realize when you're just automating posts and letting the system do the work for you. I've mentioned issues of hubris before; lots of social media marketers and PR people are quite sure that they're smarter than the average bear. Even if they are, well, that doesn't mean that said average bear doesn't notice that it's fairly unlikely that at 9:42 p.m. on a Tuesday you're on Twitter mouthing off about your brand.

"Okay, Ed," you say, "where's the danger?"

You have a few good ideas. You set up posts to publish over the next few days. You go about your day, and you forget that you've even timed them to happen. Sometimes you even let things post at random times, thinking this will get you more coverage. And then you run out of your office, patting yourself on the back for being so darn efficient, and go home to see your family and friends. And then someone responds to one of these automated posts, but you're not there to respond and communicate with them. That's bad, but it's not the worst thing that can happen.

Perhaps your unintentionally ill-worded automatic posts goes out right after some major national tragedy. Just like that, all your hard work goes down the drain. In fact, it doesn't even have to be ill worded. Your chirpy, saccharine post could be timed with tweets about a horrifying national disaster.

The Boston Marathon bombing was a major example of how poorly automated posts reflect on individuals, companies, and brands. While people were desperately tweeting to find loved ones, see whether the country was being attacked, or just generally keep up with news, fast-food companies and tech companies were tweeting inane updates. This (rightly) came off as crass and uncaring. On April 15, 2013, many people's entire Twitter streams were made up of stories, questions, and pictures about the bombings, pleas for donations to the Red Cross, and pure fear at the idea that someone could do this on American soil and so readily within such a powerful city. And occasionally within these feeds were meaningless, brand-related spittoons about exactly nothing, and the reactions toward them were venomous and disgusted.

Scotty Monty, Ford's head of social media, tweeted, "If you manage social media for a brand, this would be a good time to suspend any additional posts for the day." Food website Epicurious, somehow ignoring both common sense and Monty's advice, tweeted, "In honor of Boston and New England, may we suggest: whole-grain cranberry scones!" and received about as many negative replies as one account can receive.

However, a piece by Brandchannel (http://www.brandchannel.com/home/post/2013/04/16/Brands-Boston-Marathon-Bombing-041613.aspx) "recognized brands that have stepped up to offer support." The piece listed many tweets by brand accounts, of which I'd say only a few were actually useful. Google's landing page actively provided links about how to find people in Boston on the front page of Google.com itself. Twilio, a service software developers use to build phone- and video-call capability into apps, though at first seeming a tad mercenary, offered a "Call Your Family" app that worked on data rather than cellular lines, which are often blocked during tragedies. Vacation rental company Airbnb set up a separate service that provided (and helped individual users provide) urgent accommodations. Low-cost airline JetBlue waived flight-change plans for Boston flights and let people know that flights were still on schedule.

However, many brands simply hopped on the bandwagon. While it made *some* sense that sneaker companies ASICS America and Adidas tweeted that they were very sorry for those injured in the attacks (because people who run in marathons often wear shoes?), I question why food delivery service GrubHub had to remind people that they were doing everything they could to help diners. It's a form of ambulance chasing—trying to make some sort of profit or get attention based on a tragedy—and it doesn't look good for you. Some people might think the company has sensitive people on staff, but most will think you or your company are crass or weirdly cold.

If you're not in a position to do something tangible to help during a tragedy, I won't fault you for writing something as simple as "Our hearts go out to everyone impacted by this tragedy." But trying to slyly advertise something while doing so should get you a slap.

Your One-Stop Guide to Social Media Platforms

There is no single, perfect way to approach social media, and as mentioned, you definitely do not need to be on every single network. You should also know that no social or content network in the world is an "If you build it, they will come" situation. You will eventually have to spread your message yourself—which is time-consuming and can be a tad pathetic—and perhaps spend money on Google AdWords or advertising within that network. I know, I know, it's very sad. But that's the way of the world.

You need to think about things like where your audience is, what they like to hear, and how they like to share. Do they email back and forth, post links on Facebook, or share things on sites like Reddit or Digg? These questions will make a huge difference in determining where and how you should be devoting your energy and what you should be avoiding.

You're better off getting good at two or three and using them effectively. Here are the most well-known social media platforms you need to consider when putting together a PR strategy for your business.

Facebook

The most popular social network, even though it has become a little less exciting because of said overuse, it's still extremely relevant to your PR needs.

What you need to know about Facebook is that:

▶ It's common.

▶ It's casual.

▶ It offers opportunities for advertising and for businesses to offer products or answer questions in a way that people will actually seek out—versus need—to follow.

The most efficient way to use Facebook for your business is to set up a page for your brand or yourself. You can link this to your personal account (strictly to make it easier to administer—it won't even show as such in public), but you absolutely want to make your personal page private and keep things strictly business on the "fan page" for your brand.

Once you have developed some connections, ask them to share your page with others so you can connect with and tap into a larger community—but don't be pushy about it. This won't happen overnight, no matter what you've heard. Growing an audience takes time, patience, and diligence. Anyone who promises instant results is a scammer, plain and simple, so don't pay any attention to social media businesses that promise these kinds of results or that, worst of all, will buy followers to pad the number of people following your page. I'm not exaggerating. Lots of firms buy followers by the dozens, often just bots or shell accounts set up for the explicit purpose of padding follower counts and making something look more popular than it is.

Facebook is not only a place to post your own thoughts and news but also where you can share things from other people and use them to create conversations. Posting and sharing links, images, and videos is a great way to kick-start relevant, interesting discussions. Nothing will kill your Facebook page faster than coming across like some kind of automaton that shares only cat videos and corny inspirational memes. Furthermore, although I said your thoughts can go on your Facebook page, I heartily recommend you do not make it a stream of consciousness for your ideas. That's for Twitter, but I recommend you don't make that mistake on any social network.

As you share ideas and posts and status updates that resonate with your audience, you will begin to see more engagement and a network with accelerating growth. It can also help to reach out to the people who Facebook thinks you should connect with—hey, the buzz needs to start somewhere, even an algorithm. You may also have to pay to advertise on this platform.

If you get to the point where you find yourself dealing with the questions, comments, and complaints of your users or fans, then you're doing really well. Remember to make a concerted effort to reply to their queries, and do it with a human touch. This alone will give people a reason to keep coming back and interacting with you.

Since there's so much you can do on Facebook, you want to stick to posting a few specific things on your page. Product updates, announcements, and short, relevant thought pieces or status updates are always a good idea. Media appearances, articles written about you or your business, and anything relevant to your PR goals are also good things to post. As I said, cat videos, viral crap, and other memes are just another way to clog up people's feeds, so stay away from spamming your page with this stuff.

One of the largest issues with Facebook is that the algorithm that it currently uses does not show everything you post to everyone who likes your page. This is one way that Facebook gets you to buy impressions; it charges you money to make sure that people who already like your thing get to see it. It used to be that everything you'd post would appear, and as you'd imagine, people would see it if they'd agreed to. But now, to keep a solid Facebook following, you will most likely have to spend money.

Google+

Google+ is an acquired taste. Some say it's falling more on the minus side than on the plus side. Some say that Google has the resources to win out in the end. You may want to build something for it, but the reality is that nobody, not even Google, seems totally sure what the future of Google+ will be.

You can connect with Google+ users all over the world, and you can follow them all in a more defined way. What works well is to create a few Circles that are defined by the way they connect with your brands. For example, you might have a Networking Circle that includes people who are interested in what you have to say. But then you might also have a Circle that includes people who want to know more about the company or brand; they'll be looking for informative posts rather than chitchat. The trick with Google+ is that while the Circles allow for more security, they can also lead to confusion when it comes to how you share information. One useful feature is that you can directly post videos and photos from the Google ecosystem, including Google Drive and Picasa.

You should have plenty of things to say about your brand. Google+ is not the place to post one thing and walk away. You need to keep posting and generating new conversations. You can respond in much the same way you do on Facebook, but you will also be able to use the +1 feature for your posts so that they get exposure outside your usual Circles.

You can have multiple Google+ accounts in order to generate buzz for different brands, so it's not something that you need to create a separate business page for, like with Facebook. You can also link your Google+ page to Google Hangouts (an instant-message system that allows groups to voice or video chat), Google Docs, and all of Google's free tools. It makes good business sense to have connections integrated with the world's dominant search engine. With the right SEO keywords and a groundswell of popular conversations, well-built Google+ profiles can and will boost your brand's Google search results.

Pinterest

Pinterest is the kind of social platform that works very well for specific uses and is a total waste of time for others. If your business or brand is related to something tangible, then Pinterest is a good idea (to an extent). As an example, think of businesses such as a custom motorcycle shop, a clothing boutique, a local vegan restaurant, or a bridal store. Seriously, anything to do with weddings is a Pinterest pot of gold—one that is beautifully photographed and run through a desaturation filter.

The reason I mention this is that Pinterest is very much oriented toward visual images. In Pinterest-speak, the platform allows you to pin images to different boards that can be broken down by theme. By creating different boards, you define specific interest and market areas that will further refine your brand. This attracts audience members who share an interest in what you are doing with your brand and incentivizes them to share those specific boards, pinned posts or images, and links with a broader and similarly interested audience. If you're doing something inherently visual, something that somebody can put up and show off because it looks cool, Pinterest has immense value.

I will give you a major piece of advice before I go further, though: *Make your posts for Pinterest original.* Don't only re-post things you've just launched, and don't rehash things you've made for other networks. People will eventually (or immediately) notice and not be particularly happy. If it's something particularly, amazingly unique, you can make an exception. Otherwise, not so much.

If you are a high-end furniture company and your new coffee table is getting a lot of pins on people's interior design boards, this is a sign that not only is your strategy doing well but that you've got something that is really resonating with the public. Few other networks focus so clearly on how something looks, and few other networks can virally spread it. Instagram might offer the potential for lots of views of a single image, but Pinterest can actively spread it throughout the world.

To create that buzz, just pin the right product images from your site and re-pin things you like on your own boards. You can also like other users' pins. This is the quickest way to build followers, especially on Pinterest, where a quid pro quo relationship can develop very quickly with Pinners looking to grow their own audience. Don't misunderstand, though: there's no way to game the system to get a lot in a very short time. This, too, takes time, patience, and diligence.

To use Pinterest, just sign up with your brand's Facebook account, as this will integrate your posts with your Facebook profile. This keeps the conversation going, and it appeals to those audience members who are more visual creatures and don't just want to pore over words on a screen.

Oh, and please make sure your product images are professionally shot and look as pretty as possible. I know that your Instagram pics get tons of likes, but an iPhone photo with a retro-looking filter is *not* going to cut it. Take some of the money you're saving on PR services and hire a photographer, OK?

Twitter

Not long ago, Twitter took a back seat to Facebook as the most important social network. It still suffers a much smaller user base, but that user base is more than 250 million people. You'll definitely want to be on Twitter and have an active account that you use regularly. It's also one of the more natural social networks, where even (some) famous people (rarely) engage with their fans. Musician Andrew W.K., for example, is almost obsessively communicative with his followers, on a somewhat strange level, and there's no other network I know of where that happens.

You will want to begin with Twitter by following as many people who are related to the brand as possible. These might be people who have the same interests, gurus in the industry, or just friends of the brand. Again, you can start conversations with 140-character tweets, but then you need to follow those conversations to make sure they gain momentum. On a platform like Twitter, at the beginning, the focus is simply on building a following and reputation.

Twitter can be a rather different experience for you, depending on who you are or what your product is. If you manage a company's Twitter account, it will be very difficult for you to have a conversation with someone. It'd be like if your table started trying to have a conversation, but boring instead of frightening and hilarious. In fact, it'd come off as a tad desperate. In fact, you have to seriously consider whether you actually *want* a brand Twitter account. You may want it for Twitter's recent connection to Google results (and because it's a tad weird not to have an account at all), but you may just want to use it to make announcements into the void. People do check brand accounts simply to get updates. If you can do something interesting (for example, make Twitter-specific deals for your meat-shipment company or give out special codes for your video game), then do it. But don't invest time in it simply because you think you should.

Hashtags (denoted by the # sign) can be used to define the things you want to share about your brand. Be careful about overuse, however. Seriously, don't abuse them. Users can search for specific hashtags to refine the conversations they want to read, and spamming them with irrelevant hashtags is a great way to repel your potential audience.

Hashtags have actually become somewhat of a joke in the world of Twitter, because the truth is that you do not *need to ever use a single hashtag.* If you're tweeting while at an event or while following a live broadcast (major conferences and awards shows often have specific hashtags, such as #TheOC2016 for the Ottawa Conference on Security and Defence, or #Oscars for the Academy Awards), that might make sense. But putting five hashtags after whatever you're talking about is generally useless. (Your band just released an album? There's no need to include #album #music #band #rock.) If someone searches for a term on Twitter, it's just as easy to do so without a hashtag.

Now, to your actual tweets.

If you're a person, just be yourself—unless you're a racist, classist idiot. Then don't be yourself, and preferably log off.

Try to tweet useful things. Tweets should be funny, interesting, or newsworthy. Humor is always a big winner on Twitter, but make sure you stay within the boundaries of what's appropriate for the brand. To quote my old editor Will Porter, "Never try to be funny." This is also very, very important to apply to being intelligent and intellectual (much like normal conversation). There is nothing more insufferable than someone trying to pontificate about things in a way that isn't actually smart, good, or even new. If you see celebrities doing this and getting retweets, that's because they're celebrities. It isn't because they're smart.

Businesses should also refrain from being too saccharine. This doesn't mean you have to tweet "death is certain" every few minutes, but you shouldn't just retweet every nice thing said about you. Do it maybe twice a day. At most. While it may seem like it's making your followers feel heard, it means that anyone following you just thinks you're an inhuman, smiling garbage machine, spitting nice things at them until they agree (or unfollow you).

I do suggest that you go ahead and set up Tweetdeck or Hootsuite, two popular social media managers, and search for your brand (or your name). If you see someone say something nice, there's absolutely nothing wrong with saying, "Hey, thanks!" Since releasing my last book, I keep a column in TweetDeck that's simply a search for *This Is How You Pitch*. Yes, I get a fair number of random baseball tweets, but I occasionally catch a PR person saying something nice. I thank them, and I ask them to write an Amazon review. We foster a friendly author-reader connection, and I (hopefully) earn another review of my book.

Should you follow everyone back? Maybe. Your first instinct may be to follow everyone that comes to your Twitter doorstep, but when you do, you often end up with a quantity of followers that doesn't make sense for your or your brand's needs. If you're actually trying to *read* your feed, it also eventually becomes impossible to follow past a certain number of followers. Anything more than 2,000 and you'll be faced with a nearly constant stream of things you can't possibly respond to. If you *want* to follow that many, you should create lists or specific terms to follow, but you'll no longer be part of Twitter. You'll simply be observing it like a security console, like an episode of *Person of Interest* except that nobody you dislike gets beaten up.

To understand the accounts you're following or responding to, read a user's profile and tweets. It's that simple. To delve deeper, take a look at what other accounts that user follows. In the end, it's not about the number of people you follow but about the number of people that follow you. They need to be active and engaged in what you have to say. You want people to "Favorite" your tweets. This shows that they're not only excited by what you have to say, but they also want to come back to that link or message in the future. Being interesting and engaging is borderline impossible to teach, and any book that attempts to tell you how to do so is fighting a losing battle. All I can say is that your tweets should be interesting and entertaining in the same way that you would be in real life—except it's one, short sentence at a time.

The more that people retweet what you say, the more other people will see it, extending the message and increasing the possibility that you will gain more followers and/or notoriety. You can throw Twitter competitions as well. Give a prize to your 1,000th follower, which can grow followers briefly, but you can't guarantee they'll stick around. Give them a reason to. Oh, and whatever you do, *do not buy followers*. Someone will find out, your brand will be ridiculed, and you'll look like an ass. Sadly, I've (somewhat scientifically) noticed that people have an absolute bias toward people with 10,000 or more followers: people pay more attention to them.

Finally, there's Twitter verification. A little blue checkmark next to your handle denotes that you're the real deal, be it the real singer in a band or the real Twitter account of a brand. Twitter verification is either a case of Twitter engineers arbitrarily deciding that you're real (which is apparently based on whether people are pretending to be you but also sometimes happens when Twitter decides they like you) or of you spending $15,000 or more in advertising with them over a three-month period. It is a certain badge of honor, and it makes people think more of you for reasons that aren't immediately obvious to me. I still want one.

YouTube

YouTube isn't for everyone, even though it seems as if everyone and their mother has some kind of presence. Just because it's a great place to watch videos of kittens and people injuring their testicles doesn't mean it's right for your brand. In fact, YouTube is usually the absolute worst place to be, thanks to the site's notoriously mean-spirited users.

YouTube works best for brands with the ability to show off their product on video: tangible products in action, industry experts who can make engaging videos about their topic of expertise, and of course, those businesses that use viral videos to generate buzz (such as energy-drink companies and extreme-sports clothing brands). GoPro has done very well sharing videos from core customers and official partners.

The key to this type of curated sharing is that the GoPro team focuses on its core user base, publishing only videos that are extreme in every sense of the word. These were videos literally made with their products, making people think, "Damn, if I bought that product, maybe I could do things like that." Instead of promoting its features and superiority to other mini-camera makers, GoPro allows the product to speak volumes about its brand, establishing itself as a platform where users want to share their own videos, creating an endless amount of word-of-mouth advertising, a type of "Hey mom, look what I can do!" engagement. An estimated 6,000 videos shot with GoPro camera are uploaded every day. That powerful, endearing publicity method has paid dividends—literally. GoPro enjoys continual positive press and even had a very successful initial public offering (http://www.nydailynews.com/news/national/gopro-marketing-turns-top-youtube-brand-article-1.1875573).

When your brand wants and needs to connect via video, the goal is to make sure as many people as possible see the video and share it with others. You can share YouTube links on Facebook and Twitter, as well as on social sites like Reddit. You can also embed videos on relevant websites, blogs, and any outlet willing to share the video.

To begin using YouTube effectively, you need to set up a YouTube channel. It should contain a description of your brand, and it can be customized with brand-specific color schemes and imagery to make it more compelling. People can subscribe to the channel to get notified of new videos, essentially making them instantaneous followers of your brand's message. Your content should actually be different and enjoyable. In GoPro's case, the company had some fans who made absolutely fantastic stuff, and when the company built a significant following, it made sure to push that content to its popular, well-trafficked social media sites. This grew an even more powerful, loyal fan base. It also helps that GoPro cameras are rather foolproof to use, and from day one, the folks behind the brand knew how to bring the best possible shots, well beyond simple product demos. This involved strapping the cameras to snowboarders' heads as they shot down the slopes.

YouTube works best when you post videos that are high quality. And while you might not have a degree in film, you can still make high-quality videos for your brand with your smartphone or a small digital video camera—or you can hire a professional to do it for you. Even if you spend what you believe is the requisite amount of resources to see serious returns on a viral video, you should prepare for the inevitability that your video won't go viral. But even if it doesn't, having video content with high production values is still an important investment in your image.

Conversely, there's also some value in lo-fi video. If your product is new, and it's questionable whether it works or not, taking candid tutorial footage with a smartphone on some sort of tripod can be a legitimizing factor. I'll return once again to the Lily Camera because it applies here. The company didn't have a slick video ahead of its release to the public, so we went into one of the creators' backyards, filmed a quick demo, and uploaded the video to a private folder so that journalists could see it in action. That video also came in handy when it was time to show the public what all the hype was about.

LinkedIn

Let's be realistic here: LinkedIn is a tool for presenting the most professional side of a brand. And every brand should have a LinkedIn account, even the not-so-serious ones. LinkedIn is a place where an audience can find out exactly what a brand does, what they have done in the past, and how they are impacting the industry.

Other ways to use LinkedIn include posting status updates (keep it to a basic rundown of what the brand is working on), getting

101

involved in groups and discussions related to your industry, and of course, making network contacts.

Say what you will about LinkedIn, but it will lend a brand credibility online. It's professional, it's tame, and it is *the* site where networking happens. You can link it to your Facebook and Twitter accounts, so there is cross-posting potential as well.

Your LinkedIn profile, if it's appropriate to have one, should be honest, and it's a good idea to avoid hyperbole and overstating your achievements. LinkedIn is often, in the profile section at least, a strictly informational source. Puffery may work on some stupid people, but when a reporter is writing about you, you had best hope your information is spot-on accurate.

Significantly, LinkedIn does not afford the same anonymity as Twitter and Facebook. It is a lot more civil and professional, due to the use of real identities and because its user base is not full of basement-dwelling young men or middle-school kids. Use this rare bit of online tranquility to your advantage.

There's also a fairly strong blogging platform on LinkedIn. If you have a CEO with decent writing skills (which I'll get to), LinkedIn's influencer platform can be a great place to share content. It's also one of the few platforms where it's tolerable to chest-beat about your own successes. However, it's also full of marketing garbage. So don't expect an overnight success.

Blogs
While all social media are important in a PR strategy, blogs will still be important for a long time to come. It is also critical that you know you don't necessarily need one.

Remember that asinine phrase "If you don't have something nice to say, don't say anything at all"? In this case, you should be thinking, "If I've nothing to add, I ought to shut the hell up." Blogging and content creation should not be a requirement for your company unless you are offering specific product updates, in which case you're effectively creating a press page. If you're blogging because you like to have an opinion, be aware that until you're already very, very well established, nobody will care. In fact, even when you are, they still might not. Why sink considerable resources into something no one will read or care about?

So before you read further about best blogging practices, consider this: are you actually adding anything? Is your opinion better or more richly informed than those of other experts in your field? Do you just want a blog because other people have a blog? If the answer to that last question is "yes," please don't create a blog.

At the heart of it all, blogging is a method by which your brand can broadcast what's important. Unfortunately, there are hundreds of thousands of blogs out there, so you have to make your brand's blog really interesting, informative, and well-packaged to stand out from the rest. Make it worth something far beyond what your brand finds interesting. Think about what an audience or customer would actually want to take the time to sit down and read.

The blog might include things like:

- *Commentary about the news of the day.* Make sure that any commentary you make is actually informed by your experience and research rather than just being your take on the situation, unless you're *very* informed on it. For example, this means you were a former executive at Google and you're talking about

103

Google executives, or you're a former engineer at Google talking about how something is coded.

▶ *Longer posts about their thoughts or accomplishments.* These should be few and far between, unless you're giving (new) advice on a particular way to do something. And any story you tell about how you did something good should be layered with reality, rather than just being about how great you are.

▶ *Details about events you led or participated in.* In this case, please do not just say how great the event was. Teach the audience something.

▶ *Personal stories.* These can be great if they are deeply emotional and contain meaning. Don't just write about how you got a bagel or how a dog bit you. Write about a trying situation that you overcame—and make sure it was a trying ordeal—and poke fun at yourself. People want humanity in any personal story.

Brainstorm five things that are most important to your business. Then come up with a list of relevant blog topics that can support and encourage conversations over the long term related to those five things. Then make sure that you, as a real person with an objective opinion, would actually read and enjoy them.

If you've passed my multitude of warnings, the way to be effective with blogging is to make sure your posts appear on a consistent basis, provide value to the reader in the form of well-written information or commentary, and make the reader feel as if their comments are being read and responded to. If someone comments, respond—unless it's a troll trying to elicit a reaction, which is usually the case when someone is going for a direct insult. However, don't confuse someone making a genuine, salient point against what you had to say with a troll. You'll look stupid. There's also nothing wrong with simply not responding, unless you're dealing with libelous statements or threats, which should be noted and, if necessary, reported.

Keep in mind that blogging works only when there is enough to say and there is an even greater commitment to keep talking. The social media graveyard is littered with neglected, defunct blogs. Don't let your brand's blog be one of them.

The Truth About Going Viral

Going viral isn't something that you can make happen. There is no special recipe for making something go viral, and no company can guarantee something will get popular. In his book "Social Media Is Bullshit," B.J. Mendelson effectively spelled this out. Virality is bought through advertising or through fake followers or views on your YouTube video. Blendtec claimed "viral success," as Mendelson puts it (http://bjmendelson.com/2013/12/13/why-does-blendtec-lie-about-organic-viral-success/), for their "Will It Blend?" series of videos. In fact, their success was because they were placed on the front page of YouTube, which Mendelson claims gave them millions of views. That isn't viral success. It is an example of a big company receiving a popularity boost from another big company. This often happens with games and apps on the Apple Store, too.

In essence, you might know everything there is to know about the social networking world, but that still doesn't mean the video you created for your brand will get popular. Nothing will guarantee that. You may get lucky. You may not—unless, of course, you spend a ton of money advertising and pushing that video everywhere you possibly can.

Once you post something, sit back for a minute, grab your coffee, and see what happens next. You might hit the refresh button a few dozen times before you see anything.

You should always have a clear idea of which metrics you will use to measure the success of your social media campaigns. Is it page views, retweets, likes, shares, or comments? If you don't know beforehand, then you'll have no idea whether the time and effort you spent was fruitful.

Don't beat people over the head with what you have to say. Start with one platform, and then move the message to another and then another. You will also have to come up with new ways to share and spread the message. Your audience will get easily fatigued by seeing the same post, the same link, or the same tweet over and over again. But it's up to your wonderful creative faculties to figure out how to make that happen.

Social Media Metrics

It's easy to bogged down in all the different ways one can measure reach, exposure, and conversions on social media platforms. A good place to start measuring your campaigns is with a social media management tool such as True Social Metrics. It presents analytics across various social media platforms, allowing you to track a host of metrics, including posts, replies, shares, retweets, and pins. The key here is to keep the goal in mind: you want people to engage with your brand. It means very little that X number of people were exposed to your campaign if they did nothing when they saw it. Marketing consultant Jay Baer says it well: "The end goal is action, not eyeballs."

Here are a few ways to judge your campaign's success:

- **Conversation rate.** The number of conversations that result from any given post. On Twitter, this is replies to your tweet.

- **Amplification rate.** The rate at which your post is being shared or retweeted.

- **Applause rate.** Essentially, the number of "upvotes" you receive on a given post: Facebook's ubiquitous "Likes," Twitter's "Favorites," Instagram's "Hearts."

- **Relative Engagement Rates.** Once you've tallied responses across the platforms you're using, you can find out where your most engaged users are. This will help you determine where your time is best spent and, potentially, which social media sites to ditch.

When it comes to your blog, you can use Google Analytics and its host of tools to track specific goals, from tracking visitors to sales conversions. A whole book could be devoted to this topic, and indeed many have been. My recommendation is that if you are interested in managing (and geeking out on) these quantitative metrics, check out one of the many blogs dedicated to the topic, such as Moz Blog, which covers everything from SEO to inbound marketing.

Control the Message

While you can post the message and make sure it gets out there, you also need to be ready to do any necessary damage control. When you're controlling a message, you're looking at how it has spread and how you can make it spread in other ways. For example, if you notice that a link has been shared on a certain site, you might want to engage in conversation on that site. You may even want to bring the conversation back to your brand's site. But be careful. As I've said over and over again, audiences are very savvy, and all your work could go down the drain if your plan backfires.

For example, if someone asks a question in the comments section of an article about your company, that's a great place to step in and say, "Hey, this is the answer." However, going to that same comments section in order to address one critical comment is a silly idea if it's the only one. If there's a lot of unfair criticism (or the commenters are somehow missing some key fact), there's no problem responding and saying, "Hey, this is incorrect. Sorry, but here's the truth. And thanks so much for caring."

Controlling the message isn't about making people think a certain way, but it is about trying to ensure that the right message is getting to the right places. That kind of consistency can help your message spread faster and farther than it already has.

If you're watching the movement of the links and messages diligently, you will be the first to know when something isn't going the way you want it to. That's when your PR finesse will be needed. And to be sure, you will have times when the information is misunderstood, despite your best efforts. When this happens, you can step in, take the weight of the responsibility, and move to clear things up. If you've been consistent, you won't have to worry that you're being anything other than misinterpreted.

Press Releases

Press releases are an annoying yet necessary part of publicity. Depending on who or what you're representing, it may not be worth writing a press release. Most people do not read press releases, and most members of the media want to read only the releases related to stories they're already interested in or writing.

The state of "releasing" a press release is in the hands of companies such as PRWeb, BusinessWire, and MarketWired. Each one charges based on which wires you're using (that is, what's your geographic range or target?), whether you need the release to be translated, and whether you need to include embedded links.

A press release sent by a wire service is spammed out to any number of people. These services pad revenues by charging for extras, such as embedding links, videos, images, and social information, or by submitting to "targeted blog lists" (spamming specific people). They'll also issue a report that announces, "We placed your story in 100 different outlets!" with your release on the page of anything from a random newspaper in Arkansas to CNBC.com. The truth is that these releases are not on the actual page themselves in a place where people look. They're massive, gargantuan SEO deals to make your links appear in prominent places. That is their true value, and that value is not in generating actual news about your company. Huge companies like HP, Apple, and Sony can post releases and get press because these companies are *already* large, and people actually look out for their releases. In the case of your little startup or not-yet-a-household-name brand, you will have to weigh your options.

A press release is ideally used for informative topics rather than to sell or persuade, like an ad or a sales letter. A press release is a quasi-news story, written in the third person, by you, about your brand and in service of their goals. When done at the right time and in the right way, a press release can be helpful in a number of different scenarios:

- Introducing a new player to an industry

- Introducing a product or service

- Announcing an organizational change

Before putting any release on a wire, you should ask if what you want to announce is actually news, and you should quantify the value of a release. If you want to write it and, instead of putting it on a wire, share it with reporters, you should also really, really focus on whether this is news to them. We've gone over at length how to know that. You should also know that a press release shouldn't ever appear in your pitch; you should keep a release on hand in case a reporter asks for it.

In theory, a press release is a way of adding credibility and legitimacy to the events you're trying to publicize. Given their periodic nature, however, it shouldn't be a surprise if you don't write many press releases in a given year. It's OK. You shouldn't constantly be announcing things. In fact, you don't want to be, for a couple of reasons: if everything is a big announcement, then nothing is a big announcement, and in practice, press releases are pretty useless.

Many brands put out many press releases because they think it's something they should do, as many people in publicity do with many tasks. The truth of the matter is that most news is disseminated via pitching. Press releases don't really work without pitching. These days, press releases come in most often behind the pitch to provide all the information you didn't initially include. They're then put out on newswires, where no one reads them. One notable exception is the auto industry, where press releases are still popular. With autos, press releases are a good way to explain a lot of complex, arcane facts and figures, but this is an anomaly.

In the grand scheme of things, publicists write and release dozens of press releases on behalf of brands for the same reason they listen to their mothers and invite people they don't like to their weddings. It's expected of you; therefore, you do it.

Press Release Basics

Writing a press release is far easier than you might realize. There's even a template you can use, and I've included it below. Before you begin, look at the wire service's guidelines for press releases, just to make sure your press release conforms to expectations. Check to see what the service needs from you and what you can expect from it.

For example, if you are writing about a new product, you'll need to include the following:

▶ What it does

▶ What it will cost

▶ Where it will be found for purchase

▶ How it is better than before

▶ How it was created

Think about how you might explain a piece of breaking news to a person you've never met. If your band is releasing a new album, for instance, you might want to include when it will be released, the band's background (past albums), and sales numbers for a previous album.

Here is a template I use:

FOR IMMEDIATE RELEASE

NAME (Your Name)

NUMBER (Your Number)

EMAIL (Your Email)

MAIN TITLE FOR PRESS RELEASE
Subtitle for Press Release

(LOCATION, STATE)

It should have a basic intro saying that the company has released whatever it has released and then explaining what that thing is. It'll maybe involve a quote or two, saying how excited they are about it or who the partner involved is.

xxxxxxxxxxx press release content xxxxxxxxxxxxxxxx

xxxxxxxxxxx press release content xxxxxxxxxxxxxxxx

xxxxxxxxxxx press release content xxxxxxxxxxxxxxxx

xxxxxxxxxxx press release content xxxxxxxxxxxxxxxx

xxxxxxxxxxx press release content xxxxxxxxxxxxxxxx

(This can go on for a few paragraphs, but no more than one document page.)

###

Contact information again

That's all there is to it. This is a simple setup that allows you to express the information you hope the audience wants to hear in as clear and concise a way as possible. You may find that different press-release resources have different ideas about formatting, so double-check with them before you submit something in this format.

Five Rules for Press Releases

The basics and the template will give you what you need to write a real press release. These rules will help you write a press release someone might actually read:

1. *Don't make it longer than 400 words.* Longer releases are more expensive to put on the wire, and people's attention spans are not that long anymore. As I mentioned, your goal is to say as much as possible in as few words as you can.

2. *Don't try to be funny.* Press releases are pieces of dry, professional writing designed to convey information. Humor obscures that at times. Plus, you're probably not as funny as you think you are.

3. *Proofread it twice.* Don't ever release anything onto the wire before you've meticulously checked your spelling and grammar. Press releases make the rounds very quickly online. If the brand or the error is important enough, it could be the one mistake that follows you or your brand for a long time.

4. *Target the right media.* To make sure your pitch or press release is read, it needs to get to the places where your message will be received, heard, seen, and shared.

5. *Have something of value to share.* Without a valuable message, you may not get much traction. Find the right reporter, and let her own the story. Make her believe that you tailored your release just to her. She may still hate it, but she'll respect your effort.

Today, the public is the media and the media is your audience. The media, specifically online news outlets, are increasingly reliant on blogs, press releases, and PR campaigns for so-called content. Budgets are smaller, deadlines are tighter, and reporters are under an unprecedented amount of pressure to deliver more content—but not necessarily better journalism. This is a unique opportunity for you as a PR person. With the right approach, you can play an enormous part in influencing the message that gets disseminated. The intelligence of doing so is not in believing that the process of delivering content is done because you're so very, very clever—it's in knowing how to say something to the right person to get them to do something they already want to do.

networking

Networking, if used correctly, is one of the most powerful tools in your arsenal. You will meet all kinds of people who can help you and your clients in ways you cannot yet imagine. Your best clients, your most valuable information, and, in some cases, your most trusted friends and colleagues will come from networking in one way or another. Almost any career that involves money changing hands involves some sort of networking element.

What you need to know is how to do it properly. Too many people think networking is about shaking hands, handing out business cards, and calling on people only when you need a favor. That is the worst way to go about it.

The notion that a good network is all about relationships may seem elementary, but that crucial concept is lost on most people. They think it's all about "What can others do for me?" and "How can I get them to do it?" In fact, it's the opposite. If you're just a person worth talking to, someone worth discussing something with in person, or a respite from the hell of an event created to pinball people into each other, you're more likely to succeed than the slimeball to your right.

If you haven't already noticed, I'm a big fan of using examples of what *not* to do as a way of showing you how you should approach certain PR-related topics.

If you have your own business, startup, or anything else that makes money, you already have some understanding of how networking is done. If you didn't, you wouldn't have gotten funding from your investors, sold any of your products, or done any of the things required to make a living in this world. But all your networking has probably been in the context of business-to-business interaction. What about when you have to deal with the media and other people who are in a position to help you but aren't necessarily customers? Or what about situations where you haven't thought ahead about your actions?

If you're a remarkably attractive man or woman, I really do not advise you to, mid-conversation, walk away because someone better is available and you want a chance to talk to him or her. I've seen a very well-put-together PR person end a lengthy conversation (people-watching is my form of medication at these events) the moment that someone important walked by, like a dog who just saw its favorite toy sail past.

In any case, people have memories. Long memories. Especially people that get jilted because someone better came along. Reporters change outlets or get promoted, and they will almost certainly remember a moment like that. I'm not saying every (or even many) PR person, male or female, is using sex appeal to get ahead. What I am saying is that any level of "Oh, wait, sorry, someone more important has come along, I must go" will probably fail you in a spectacular fashion.

Honesty can work. You can say, "Oh, shit, that person over there? For four years, I've been trying to get some face time. Can I go talk to him and find you immediately afterward?" If you keep your promise and find that person afterward, that's just fine. It's the same net result without the jilting.

The key is to *not use people*. If you don't like someone, don't force yourself to hang out with him. Don't laugh at his jokes if he's not funny. If you're not his number-one fan, don't force it. Be friends with people you like. There will be the rare but inevitable situation where you don't like somebody but you have to put up with him, lest you end up in a situation with potentially negative consequences. You'll be able to tell when this is happening because it will feel like you don't have a choice. That's when you have to be a professional and suck it up. Otherwise, life is too short for shitty people. You don't have to sit there and take someone being rude to you, either; just walk away if you hate it. Just be honest.

Your best contacts will almost never be able to help you right away, at least not in any tangible sense. You'll meet them somewhere (often in the most unexpected places), find you have something in common professionally, and then bond over something personal. It might be a hobby, a shared cultural background, or taste in food, art, or music. When you meet somebody and think "That's someone I want to keep in touch with" for reasons that have nothing to do with the business of PR, that's when you can be sure they will be one of your most valued connections. In fact, most really great networking is done through avoiding business entirely, because anyone who just launches into business discussion is really weird and boring. Then again, there are situations where you'll meet someone who only wants to talk business, but they're rare enough these days that you probably don't need to deal with them. If you do, just . . . well, talk about business. It'll probably be a tad boring.

You must be open to discovering that relationship. It isn't something that happens to you. It happens because of, and with, you. More importantly, for our purposes in this section, make sure you nurture that relationship. Email the person you liked so much, or call her up (if you must), and take her out for coffee, a drink, or dinner.

Obviously, do not show up unannounced at her place of employment or home and ask to hang out. Obviously, don't pester her, but try to keep the relationship strong. Imagine that you're new in town and she's one of your first "native" friends. If someone doesn't respond to your coffee request after two or three tries over a month or two, then assume she doesn't want to hang out. It's not you, or her. It's just the way of the world.

I am a proponent of networking the old-fashioned way—getting out there, meeting people, and keeping up some semblance of a personal life—rather than networking via a million anonymous social media contacts. If you consider your networking to be friends with the vague benefit of having some business aspect you can use as a very small tax deduction, you'll go farther than the gung-ho manipulators of the world.

The Power of a Good Network

Second in importance only to being able to pitch, having a solid network of contacts is key. Think about the benefits of a good network:

▶ More power

▶ More influence

▶ More opportunities to spread the word about you and your client

▶ More opportunities to make connections

In a broad sense, a good network is a tool for growing your PR prowess. The more people you know, the better you're known, the more you can do, the more clients you can get, and the more connections you can make. On the other hand, a bad network won't promote your brand, won't return your calls, and won't help you or your clients prosper. The key to a good network is the right connections. Without them, your network is like a tree without a root system. It won't grow, it definitely won't spread, and it will eventually wither away. Of course, try not to think about it as a giant thing you can master, like some kind of oversized bonsai, but more as a weird community garden that everyone tends together and sometimes sprouts useful things that make your professional life better.

Having the right connections also matters when things don't go the way you intended professionally. A good network can create support for your next move when the previous one was a misstep. Solid connections can step in and speak up for you. They can make sure things don't get worse, sometimes even reversing the trend. They can help you get a call answered in the right place, help soften a blow to you, or even warn you that something is coming just before it hits you square in the unmentionables.

A network can be a lifesaver.

How to Treat the People Who've Helped You

Everybody wants to feel like they make a difference in the lives of those they work with. Even more, everybody loves to be recognized for it. When you have a loyal audience or network that has seen you through the peaks and valleys of life, you need to show your gratitude. That gratitude is like sunlight and rain, nourishing your growing PR empire.

Find ways to publicly thank those who deserve it. From a client perspective, even something as simple as a social network post about how grateful you are for having loyal supporters can go a long way. New converts to your brand feel extra good about being recognized.

And from there, they are often even more vocal in their support for future endeavors.

A Note on Written Notes

I have a killer secret I use when I really want to go the extra mile for somebody. When I want them to know just how much I appreciate them I—wait for it—write them a note. I should add that I have dyspraxia, a developmental coordination disability that means my handwriting is more akin to a very bad drawing than to words. Thus, I type out notes, sign them, and usually write something short on the back so they know I'm not just form-writing. However, there's a power to the written, sent letter that few know.

It is a simple gesture that takes little additional time or effort, and it absolutely blows people away. Nobody writes notes anymore. It's a relic of a more genteel era when people actually gave a shit about etiquette and manners.

If you want to be really slick about it, get some stationery or letterhead made. Most stationery shops will do thank-you notes with your name printed on very nice paper stock. Letterhead is more for business correspondence, but it can work. Write something short and from the heart. And although most of your pitches and emails will be discarded, people tend to keep notes as mementos. Your goal is that a few people keep this gesture in their memory banks.

The truth is, even a nice thank-you email matters. I don't recommend sending one to every reporter who writes a story about your client or you. However, if they write something about you that really changes your life or makes you feel warm inside, then say that. Be genuine.

Most people just simply don't say "Please" and "Thank you." Remember that.

Rebuilding Fractured Relationships

It's imperative that you treat everyone with as much respect and decency as possible. This is important for two reasons: you're trying to establish the best possible reputation for your brand, and you're always trying to build and grow your network. Acting like an asshole or treating people with disrespect jeopardizes both of those.

Being a good person doesn't mean everything will go smoothly 100 percent of the time, of course. You will have encounters that don't go the way you wanted them to or people who don't react the way you expected them to. This can happen frequently with members of the media. You gave a reporter bad info, or you gave someone else the scoop you promised him. Even though you need to be on your best behavior when you're in PR, you are still human, and you will make mistakes. It happens. There's also the important point to remember that even the most saintly, calm creatures in the world will occasionally slip up and be an asshole. This includes me, except far more often than I'd care to admit. I have a slightly more abrasive personality than most, and while it's helped me get where I am, it also means I've buggered up my fair number of situations.

If your client can't understand this—or you can't understand this—you're in the wrong business. Think about what might happen if your client makes a mistake. Do you immediately give up on them? No. You try to fix things. That mostly means being honest and understanding all the details you can.

I once had a client working in the home-improvement industry. I had booked a trip to Florida for a few days, and I neglected to tell him. When he kept calling me during the trip, I wasn't up front that I was actually gone; I was scared what he'd think. Eventually, I came clean. The relationship was never the same, and it fell apart a few months later. It would have been really easy for me to say "Hey, [client], I'm taking a vacation for a few days like normal human beings do." I don't know if he'd have reacted well or badly to it, or asked for money back for the days I was gone. If he had been mean, well, then I'd have not wanted to work with him anyway. Nevertheless, I wasn't honest, and I paid dearly. As I write this part of the book, I'm sitting in Hawaii on vacation, and all my clients know where I am and when I'll be back.

My honesty even netted future business. While away, I'd canceled all my calls, but one person—a new business prospect—said it would mean the world to him if I'd chat for 15 minutes. I acquiesced. When I got to my room, he'd sent a pair of cocktails and a handwritten note. Honesty is the best. (Months later, the moral of the story is not just that I got a free drink out of the deal. The client signed, he was very happy with my services, and we worked together for many fruitful months. The end.)

Just remember to be honest about whatever happened. Don't try to rationalize or justify. You won't learn from those mistakes otherwise. Instead of wallowing in a pit of despair, soaked in vodka, think about what went wrong and how you might handle things differently in the future. If you're really swimming in emotional hell, I advise writing down exactly what happened, as if it were a timeline, and figuring out what you could have *reasonably done*, objectively—as if someone other than you were living it.

Say "Sorry." Mean It.

Did you say something snarky? Check in with whoever is upset with you. Find out from them what happened and what they think went wrong. You may find out that you didn't actually do anything wrong and that they were just having a bad day. The more information you can get, the more you can learn moving forward. If you did screw up, take responsibility for it. Let the upset party know that you realize you could have handled things better and that it won't happen again. Ask them what you can do, *anything within reason*, and if they respond positively, try your best to do it. Don't be saccharine or pathetic. Just be up front that you truly care about what happened and that you didn't want it to go wrong.

Make sure you offer a sincere apology. Even though you might think you'll save more face if you just move on, this is not what others want to hear. Most people love apologies, and most people aren't given them. In business it's very common to find people attempting to avoid a real apology, even more so than in real life. The most common one is "I'm sorry you feel that way."

Let's deconstruct that sentence. It has two components: an apology ("I'm sorry") and an immediate removal of said apology ("you feel that way"). It means, "I'm not sorry for what I did, but I am sorry that you are unhappy." It does not accept blame or responsibility, or even say that you care. It says that you are sorry they had a feeling. It is a non-statement, a vulgar aberration of the human language, and it has become so common that you will hear anyone from a 14-year-old to a 75-year-old utter it in a multitude of scenarios.

Say that you're sorry about what happened, say that you are specifically sorry for your part in it, and ask what you can do to fix it. Honestly, there will be situations in which there isn't something you can do. Just know your soul is clean.

Depending on the situation, send something along if you really mucked things up. A reporter may not be the best target for this, as different outlets have many different ethical guidelines. (One reporter

I know won't even accept a glass of water at an event.) However, a card or something stupidly small like a chocolate bar won't be harmful. Flowers and fruit baskets can be too large and too ridiculous. Flowers from a male PR person to a female reporter can be seen as romantic (and thus very creepy). For a young male reporter, perhaps it's a six-pack of a beer you know he likes and a note: "I messed up." Learn your audience.

In any case, you'd be shocked by how few people try to make amends for their wrongdoings, let alone make a gesture expressing regret. A sincere, heartfelt phone call is also always appreciated, *though many reporters still don't like phone calls.*

What We Talk About When We Talk About Networking

Nobody in their right mind should ever, ever approach a networking event with the express goal of "networking," even though most people do. You should treat any interaction—be it an organized networking event, a lunch or dinner with someone you want to meet and talk to, or an unplanned introduction—like any other social event. With one major difference: you must be prepared.

By that I mean you need to be able to talk shop, and talk about anything but that. And know when it's time to switch between the two topics.

Do Your Research

I advise newly established PR types to do their research on their clients, the industry they are working in, their client's competitors, and all points in between. You need to do the same.

Not only will it help you in the course of your everyday business activities, but it gives you lots of talking points to use during these situations. For you, the overarching goal is making contacts with people who are in a position to talk about your brand or product. And any reporter, blogger, writer, or producer worth their salt will not only be sizing up what you are all about, but also working on their own stories, likely about competitors or developments in your field. They'll also be, if they're at this event, beset by people forcing stories down their throats or only wanting to talk shop.

Some of the best advice I can give any business or PR professional is not to immediately launch into a conversation about what they do and what they want from the person they're talking to. It's the equivalent of screaming, "HEY, WANNA GO BACK TO MY PLACE?" a few minutes into talking to someone at a bar. You need to learn the ebbs and flows of a conversation and adapt as necessary.

Want to be someone worth talking to? Gently solicit their feelings on something you've been reading or learning about. See what their beat is, and talk to them about it. Ask them what their favorite information sources are or who they think is an authority on your field. That's if you're out for coffee with them. At an event, it's worth letting them talk, letting them lead the conversation entirely, and talking about what they want to talk about. A reporter at an event is like a woman at a speed-dating event with four hundred men who have never been on a date. They will appreciate the respite from someone immediately demanding something from them. They may even like the conversation.

If you're well read, researched, and informed, you might be able to offer an informational tidbit, a new angle, or maybe even the holy grail of reporting: inside information (if you're talking business, that is).

Apart from actually being an interesting and fun-to-talk-to human being, nothing makes you unforgettable to a journalist like having good information. The reporter in question may not write about your product for a million different reasons, but she might call you for a quote (which still gets your name out there), give you a tip about something she heard, or refer you to somebody better suited to covering your client.

Don't Talk Shop Too Much

Of course, you never have license to spout off like a know-it-all, no matter how well informed or intelligent you are. You also don't want to be some freak automaton who is capable of talking *only* about work in the most one-dimensional way possible.

You need to strike the right balance between talking about personal and professional matters. By personal, I do not mean asking people about how much money they make or what their favorite position is.

You can talk about golf, cooking, and other hobbies and make polite small talk, but you can and should also dig a little deeper, especially with reporters. Find out if they have a family, what their career history was like (most reporters started their careers at small-town newspapers and have some great stories about that), or really anything that can help you connect on a level that doesn't seem like you're just there to get their business card and hit them up when you need something. Some of the finer details, like whether they have children or whether they volunteer at an animal rescue, will help you determine whether you should invite them out for drinks (probably a bad idea if they have to put their kids to bed) or perhaps breakfast or lunch. (And if you invite them to drinks, make sure they drink.) Don't be afraid to be honest about a recent event that didn't go as planned or about something weird about your job. Don't trash-talk what you do or your clients, but your conversations with other human beings outside work are usually not entirely positive or entirely about one thing and entirely about the things you love. Networking follows this same pattern; so talk to other people you meet as if they are what they are: fellow human beings.

Good reporters (and other media types) are trained to sniff out bullshit, and if you act like a slimy, self-serving asshole, they'll not only figure it out right away but immediately think of you negatively. Good luck getting a meeting with them or an email returned.

I often use the dating analogy to describe PR tasks, but only because it's so apt. If you meet somebody who is self-important, endlessly promoting their new venture, and spouting off all kinds of jargon with a complete one-track mind, you probably wouldn't call them back—if you even got that far. So why would you act that way with someone you're trying to professionally court?

And in the same way that you generally don't push to have sex on the first date, you should *never* lead with the sale. Remember that you're there to have a good time, get to know the other person, and see if you want to get together again.

Yes, there will be times when you have a few precious moments to pitch someone really important. I know someone who once saw a famous venture capitalist at a stoplight, rolled down his window, pitched the investor, and ended up getting an obscene amount of money for his new app. That isn't remotely the norm, though, and you might use that beautifully fortuitous moment to screw up your one big chance.

Some of my best conversations with reporters and clients have been about nothing remotely related to our work. Ultimately, it always comes down to your ability to do what you say you're going to do, but if you're an interesting-enough person to have a conversation with, that will help you go a few extra miles.

Being an interesting person isn't something you can really teach, especially if you're not a naturally curious person. But broadening your horizons will help you become a better person, as well as a better interview subject.

It seems trite to suggest it, but read something new. Poetry. Literature. Non-fiction. It doesn't really matter. To become interesting, consume culture, listen to new music, and watch comedy and weird things that you might not usually watch. This does not mean you need to become a renaissance man or woman, but you might be surprised by the number of people in any industry who simply can't talk about anything other than their work. It's pretty easy to stand out when you're the only person in the room with any notable hobbies or an ability to ask others meaningful questions about something other than work.

Attending Networking Events

Here's a simple way to tell whether you should go to a networking event. If you have to sign up for it, don't go. Similarly, if the event costs money and the money doesn't go to charity, skip it—especially if it's being thrown by a marketing or PR agency.

Most of these events are moneymaking schemes or populated by the kind of person I told you *not* to be in the above chapter. You really, really need to avoid these events, as well as these people.

So how do you spot a good networking event?

You'll probably have to be invited to it, and not through some Facebook event post, either. This will be a handpicked crowd of people that the host thinks will be relevant to one another. Fewer than 50 people is a good rule of thumb, and ideally, you'll know someone who is attending.

This is a good environment to get shit done, since it will be a small, relatively intimate gathering, with the participants already vetted by the host. It also won't be held at some noisy reception hall or cool "event space" filled with loud music and dark lighting, two major killers for any professional networking event.

Two's a Crowd

Unless you're more confident than most, networking can be quite intimidating. In essence, you are in a room of people you either don't know at all or know only in a professional context. Occasionally, you'll have friends, but more often this serves as a crutch and makes it easier to avoid the task of going out and making connections with new people.

It's important you for you to correctly read the room and any conversations going on. When you walk in, you'll probably see a few groups of people talking. If it's two people talking and they seem to be genuinely engaged in their conversation, you may see this as an opportunity to "add" to their discussion. The truth is, if two people are talking, and they're interested in the conversation, any impromptu comment will likely be seen as an unwelcome intrusion.

A great example of this is when I was at another PR firm's event with a reporter friend of mine. We were having an animated conversation about comics. A loud, annoying PR person sat next to us and attempted to add superhero-related content to our conversation, which came off as a try-hard interruption. The person quit while he was ahead, when he understood he had nothing to add, and then walked away. I admit this may have been because I went into an insufferable, animated rant about how *Batman Begins* is the best Batman movie based on D.C. comic history. While my friend laughed and enjoyed it, the intruding publicist got a bit weirded out and left.

Of course, there are those situations where you'll find someone desperately bored, potentially with a look of horror, with the person she's stuck talking to. This can be tough to judge, but a commonality is when you see them standing silently for longer than five minutes or looking around for an emergency exit. This can be a great time to step in and save the person from death by boredom. You can simply say something completely unrelated or stand to the side, between them, and interject when appropriate.

Three's a Party

If three or more people are standing around, it's most likely a group conversation, where you might able to add something. As ever, my advice is to determine whether you'll be able to add something funny, interesting, or useful to the conversation. Again, talk like a normal human being. This isn't something I can teach, but don't be afraid to pick up a book or newspaper to see what's going on outside your head. If you're at an industry event, then you can talk about what's happening in the industry. This isn't to say you should blurt out "So did you hear about that terrible news, eh?" since that comes off as desperate and weird. Simply add to what is being discussed something that others will think insightful or apt.

If you can't find a natural break in the cadence of a conversation, it's probably because those people are already friends or are in the process of becoming friends. Your presence may not be welcome at that time. If you must, stand around them with your drink, and wait your turn. Most people aren't rude enough to go on chatting for too long without involving a person who has been standing silently for the duration of their conversation. Eventually, you'll be asked who you are and what you do, and then hopefully you'll be able to be part of their conversation. If it doesn't happen, which is possible, then you won't be able to network with these people, and you move on. No big deal. They could all be complete jerks, and that's not your fault.

The real trick to networking in person (as opposed to spamming people on LinkedIn) is that you should be a person who can just talk to people. It sounds so simple, doesn't it? Most people have something that you can talk to them about. I would argue that if you find someone boring, it is usually more your fault than theirs. It won't always be a smooth conversation, but the more you practice, the better you will become at uncovering what makes people tick and getting them to talk about themselves and their interests.

If you're scared, that's natural. People are scary. Not being wanted is scary. Getting rejected is scary.

Let's Get Rejected!
You should be ready for rejection at every turn. There, I said it. For every person at an event, there is someone who can and will hurt your feelings. One time, I was at an event at a law firm and met the notable venture capitalist Jason Calacanis. He had recently written a newsletter in which he ripped into one of my clients. I went up to him and jokingly mentioned the piece, saying we appreciated the feedback (which we actually did). He stood there and proceeded to rip my client apart again, all while gesturing toward me and laughing. The rest of the conversation he did everything he could to cut me down. It was one of the single most humiliating experiences in

my career. It also taught me, after some meditation on the situation, that it doesn't matter who someone is, how much money they have, or what fancy position they hold.

Rude is rude. Someone who clearly enjoys making someone else feel bad is, at the very least, rude. They're also probably not someone you want to be your business partner or friend.

That experience caused me to avoid events for a long while. But I did eventually get back on the horse to ride into battle. Sometimes, at events, I would still meet people who would outright say, "Ugh, whatever, you're in PR." But it didn't sting nearly as badly as it had before. And eventually, I learned through these unpleasant interactions to stop talking about my work and instead focus on making solid friends and contacts at networking events.

It was an important shift for me, and if you're struggling with networking, it might change your experience as well. When I started talking to others like people instead of potential colleagues, I wasn't dependent on making people like me based on my job or theirs. Instead, I was able to focus on meeting random people who would be fun to know in general, and maybe later on make some sort of business connection. If you approach networking events with this mindset, you actually have a much greater chance of making a new business contact.

People still say, "Ugh, you're in PR," but now I usually just say, "I know, right? It's like you just saw roadkill come back to life." I don't mind insulting my career. PR is kind of stupid.

You're Going to Die

By far the best lesson in life you can learn is the "death is certain" principle.

Now, this doesn't mean you should walk into the room and kill someone or yourself. What it means is that we all eventually die. It doesn't matter if you're a famous venture capitalist, a farmer, an NFL linebacker, or a shy person at a networking event. From the moment we enter into this world, the hourglass is turned. This sounds brutal and scary, but really, it is liberating. In this way, we are all equals.

If you see someone you want to speak to, then do it. Feel your heart racing, the cold sweat start to run down your forehead, the physical manifestation of the fear of rejection. You have it in your power to ignore all of this and remember that someday you'll be resting six feet underground, as will they. You are equals. Breathe deeply, walk over, and introduce yourself.

Most people at networking events are desperate. They want something from someone, be it money, press, or both. The best way to get what you want is to befriend someone honestly and connect with them the way you would with a normal person. When you approach someone, even if they are well known, you will often find that most people aren't that difficult to talk to. Most people will just be happy to have a conversation about something that isn't related to whatever the event is about.

If someone is brusque and doesn't want to talk, don't bother forcing it. If someone is being rude to you, just eject yourself politely, because life is too short. It's also natural to feel terrible after this, but don't let that make you feel like you're less of a person. I can't say this enough: no matter how important someone is, either there's a reason they acted like that or they're just a bastard.

If someone wants to talk only shop, you can do that, too. The trick is to get into the flow of the conversation. When you remember you are going to die, you can forget about holding back your opinions or trying to be too diplomatic. If someone is deadly quiet, they're probably either in sheer awe of you (unlikely) or totally and utterly bored (more likely). It's a funny moment to ask the other person if you are boring. If they say yes, tell them I said to piss off.

Perhaps the dark secret that is hiding out in the open is that most people don't want to be at these events. Very few people actually enjoy "networking," in big quotation marks. The ones who do are largely useless to you. They are not reporters or famous CEOs. The people who are there to see and be seen are like vultures ready to descend on any scrap of meat they catch a whiff of. You'll know them quickly because they will drop their company's name and their position before you have a chance to look for your escape route.

Networking Online

Following the dating analogy, in the past few years it's become far more acceptable to connect with people online—and we're thankfully past the "I just want to get laid" stage. Much of this has to do with our growing acceptance of the role technology plays in our lives and the fact that people seem more comfortable making the first step of an interaction online. If used properly, networking through social media can put you in touch with a range of people you could have only dreamed of 20 years ago.

Your Profile

To start, it can be tempting to put up a glossy front to hide your blemishes. Everyone tries to put their best foot forward online, and this can come off as uninteresting. Avoid boring, but avoid blatant lying, too. While it may work for some people, I prefer honesty, and anything I do online is an extension of my personality, not what I hope people perceive me to be.

When it comes to crafting your profile, I don't advise being either funny or overly professional. My Twitter profile is a slight exception in that I make one joke: "The best PR twitter," referring to a list on which I was #1 for PR tweets (which I thought was ridiculous). I then follow with very basic information: "British. PR. @Inc Columnist. Media Relations. Author of #1 Bestseller *This Is How You Pitch* http://ran.do/book." That's it. I'm British, I do PR, I write for Inc., I do Media Relations, I have a bestseller, and here's the link. No smoke and mirrors.

A common mistake is the generic nonsense that publicists put in their profiles. "PR Professional" or "social media marketing genius" or "blogger" or "I love to run and drink coffee." If you mention in your Twitter profile that you drink coffee or run, or even if you talk about what you "love," you'll come across as twee, generic, and ignorable. You're one of many. Your profile will not get someone to say, "I must be on this person's radar!" It should be purely informational. Oh, and never, ever use a quote.

If you're not a publicist, put what you do—and that's it. I really mean that. Someone going to your profile is there to find out who you are or how to get in touch with you. If they can't find that, or they find things that make them dislike you, then you've shot yourself in the arse.

Getting in Touch via Social Media

My preferred outlet for "networking" online is Twitter. I put that in quotation marks because you should be approaching it from the perspective of actually socializing. Twitter is a stream of people discussing things with each other, making stupid jokes, posting things they wrote, and reposting what others have written. Post things that are relevant and interesting to you. Retweet the things you like. Twitter is not a place where you have to say something for the sake of proving you are present; it's a place where you're talking to people who share an interest with you. Imagine that interacting on Twitter is like chatting people up in a bar or a weird coffee shop.

The same line of thinking for face-to-face networking applies to the sphere of social media. Be yourself. When you talk to people, have an actual conversation. I can't teach you how to be interesting, but I can teach you to say what you are thinking. If your thoughts are that a reporter's article was bad, perhaps you it's best to avoid saying, "Your article sucked." Rather, you'd say, "I don't know if I agree on X point." If he responds, happily discuss it in a conversational manner. Be careful not to step into waters you don't have the intellectual backing to enter, and good lord, if you're a man, don't step in and argue with a woman about her health choices or major life decisions. That's 100 percent not your lane, and it will only make you come across in the worst possible way.

When you like someone's article, your first idea may be to say something overly agreeable to him or her. Tweeting something such as "Oh, great article on xyz!" comes off as banal and won't make them like you. You will get lost in the sea of unimpressive and ignored tweets. I would recommend telling him or her the specifics and asking a pointed question. For example, a reporter for the *Wall Street Journal* who does a great number of videos actually decided to follow me back because I was, over time, specifically complimentary on the quality of her videos. This wasn't a lie, either, because her work is actually stellar.

Taking a step back, the best way to research a reporter is to read what they write. Once you know that, follow their Twitter, but don't respond to everything they say. It's very important not to come off as desperate, even if you are desperate for their attention. This is partly because there are thousands (or tens of thousands) of people bothering them all day for their attention, their adulation, and in the case of a publicist, their ability to write things about their clients so that they keep getting paid. Don't add a reporter on Facebook, either. I consider it a no-fly zone for work in general. It's invasive, and it will come off as creepy. A reporter doesn't want to be sharing photos of their children with you just because you are hoping to get some press coverage from them.

Whatever you do, even if you ignore all my advice, do *not* use Twitter as a pitching ground. This is extremely important. At most, Twitter is a place to lay a foundation with someone. As I've mentioned, a big strength is being able not to talk about your work. Look at this as an opportunity to publicly present yourself as a person who isn't just another automaton dribbling out words promoting how great they are. Twitter is a professional and personal space where you can both grumble about and enjoy things with other people. There are exceptions (Farhad Manjoo of the *New York Times* actually *prefers* direct-messaged pitches on Twitter), but they are few and far between, and you should assume that no reporter wants to receive private messages from you on Twitter.

I was tweeting about trying to manage and track my medication recently when a young PR person responded to my tweet with a link to her client. She represented a client with an applicable product—a good product, in fact, one that I'm glad I found. This isn't necessarily a bad thing to do once or twice, especially if it's the perfect fit. (And it really was!) However, it made me dig into her Twitter history, and I found that in the previous few months she had been working on an app that creates awful-looking Photoshops out of images you have on your phone. She had been responding to reporters' jokes with these terrible images. None of the reporters had responded—except one, who wrote, "Haha, thanks!" The PR person, in a move that truly confused me, responded with another terrible, poorly rendered Photoshop of that person in a space suit, with the words "Check your email." This meant she wanted the person to check his email, invariably for a pitch she'd sent.

This wasn't just embarrassing in how consistently it showed how bad the photo edits were (and by extension, the app she was clearly trying to promote); it also was invasive, somewhat akin to a stalker putting their face next to yours and drawing on little hearts. I tweeted at her that what she was doing was poor practice and a little creepy, and she never responded. I'm guessing her boss thinks she's a "new media guru" and a "real go-getter."

My point is that the key to public relations success is not trying too hard. It is especially relevant online since it leaves a more permanent impression and is often the first point of contact these days for people who have never met you. If you consistently find that reporters aren't responding to your tweets, it shows that they are not particularly interested in what you are offering. Slow down and be mindful of whether your approach is truly working. Because even if you win the rat race, you're still a rat.

Networking with the Press

Here's the big thing about the press: When presented with someone who wants them to write about something, most will not be particularly happy. Of course, they know the game, and some will play along with it; however, I don't suggest you approach it from this angle. My play with reporters is to never, ever mention my clients unless they specifically ask me what I'm working on. For me, it's common courtesy and respect for another's profession.

An excellent "trick" is to ask them if there is anything they are interested in hearing about. I email them this question: "What do you want me to send you, if anything?" In the subject header I'll say that this is not a pitch. You should also say that you read their coverage (this should be true), and hopefully they'll tell you what they want to hear about. Feel free to ask them questions. If they don't tell you, well, that sucks, but you tried to find out what they might like. That's a fairly good way of finding out what to pitch them—finding that square hole for the square peg you work for.

If you have the opportunity to meet with a reporter or blogger, I advise you to chat with them with about themselves, again focusing on being a normal human being who has normal, interesting conversations. Remember that people in the press will know you have an agenda. If, or when, they ask you what you're working on, answer in the most normal and approachable way possible. Talk about it with the hype scraped off, leaving you with just the honest facts and benefits of whatever it is you're pushing. Keep the barrier between friendship and professionalism up. You can be both, but don't expect them to publish just because you are friends. You shouldn't be friends with them for the sake of work, either. That's manipulative and sociopathic, and all too common in PR.

A Note on Mentors

Finding people to help and mentor you in the PR industry can be hellish. Many people are scared that if they share their insider secrets or contacts, they'll be overtaken by the next generation. It's not to say it's impossible to find a mentor, but a lot of senior people in public relations tend to have their guard up.

As a general rule, if you're kind, eager, and competent, people will want to help you. Publicists who land press do so because they are well connected, and it's never a matter of saying to someone, "Hey, go get well connected." It takes introductions and knowing things that you can't learn without relations to people farther down the path. I've mentored 15 people, of whom about 10 have turned out pretty well. The five who fell to the other side did so because they didn't manage all the different tasks it requires to get press, much of which we've covered in this book: reading a lot, knowing certain things, and being a good, approachable human.

Some of the best mentors in PR will be journalists. Roberto Baldwin, a reporter for the technology website Engadget, said at a panel I organized that he would gladly walk into any agency and tell them how to pitch him. That's a common perspective: most reporters will happily mentor you in how to deal with them. In the greater scheme of PR and marketing, if you contact someone who works in house at a company you admire, they'll be less likely to assume you're a threat (unless you're working for a competing product).

Do your best to learn from people who are actually succeeding, as judged by the client's actual results, or learn from the reporters they are pitching.

media preparation and crisis communications

t's my sincere hope that the lessons in this book have helped you get attention from the media and will not be used to light a fire when your plane crashes in the Andes and you have to resort to cannibalism to stay alive. If you haven't taken anything from these lessons, then I've failed in my mission to help make the PR industry irrelevant (or make you better), and I should be the first one to be eaten.

But what if you have actually put my lessons to good use? All of a sudden, you've got reporters, bloggers, and the odd TV producer hitting you up for interviews and sound bites. Reporters want to profile you. Finally, you're in a position where media relations is another matter that you need to deal with.

Despite what our culture tells us, not everyone or everything was meant to be on TV or plastered all over our newspapers and magazines. This doesn't necessarily mean that you are ugly, stupid, or lacking charisma. If you've already built a business or brand for yourself, you've obviously got something going that has made people like you enough to give you startup money, buy what you're selling, or bring you as far along as you are. Some excellent companies have had some quite boring people at the helm and still managed to land excellent media coverage.

But that doesn't mean you are meant to be in the spotlight. Have you ever tried acting? You may have had the looks and the social skills to be the coolest guy or girl in school, but in drama class, one of the theatrical elite probably made you look like a bumbling dork. That's because acting well is *really* hard. That's why good actors get paid well for doing so.

Being interviewed, especially on television, is similar to acting. You need to remember your lines, which in this case are facts about the product or talking points about your brand, and have a general grasp on how to respond to questions. As with great actors, it's more than simply remembering the lines; you'll also be judged on delivery. You need to be able to deal with improvisation, whether it's a curveball question or steering the conversation. And you need to keep your composure at all times. There's nobody yelling, "Cut!" and no re-dos. Oh, and try not to sweat through your makeup.

Once again, this will require preparation on your part. Steve McQueen didn't just walk into Hollywood and star in *The Great Escape*. He took classes with Lee Strasberg, the greatest acting coach of his day. While the whole point of this book is to put the PR powers back in your hands, you may want to invest in some media training. Unlike most PR people, media trainers have, as Liam Neeson says, a very specific set of skills, ones that are quite difficult to deliver in a book even if you *do* have them.

The greatest media trainers often assist government officials, military leaders, captains of industry, and all sorts of people who are more important than you are and who are playing for much higher stakes. You must remember that the greatest people in any industry steal talents from others, and thus working with trainers who don't necessarily train people in your sphere of influence might actually be powerful. There's a great educational value to being told, "To everyday people, what you just said sounded stupid."

Be a Good Guest

The number-one rule of any interview with the media—on the phone, on a podcast, in the street, on a bus, wherever—is to be a good guest. You are selling yourself as an interesting person and a good interview subject, which will in turn make people interested in what you have to sell or promote. Even if you're talking about your product because they want to write about it, you still need to be interesting enough to warrant the conversation.

Think about it. If you're a musician and Pitchfork asks you for your top 10 albums of the year, would you list your own as number one, let alone as one of the top 10?

Of course not. It's hard to imagine a more stereotypically arrogant thing to do. Trying to flog your own brand in the middle of an interview is a similarly boorish play.

But if you give funny, thoughtful, or interesting answers to the reporter's questions, you'll come off well. Weezer frontman Rivers Cuomo, even though his band's albums have progressively gotten worse, regularly gets press by saying interesting albeit kooky things and by being available to the press. This has helped him escape the doldrums of his band's critical flaying.

Offering useful, interesting, or attractive content for readers means that when the reporter mentions you and your product or service at the end of the interview, you *will* have people looking you up and seeing what you're all about. You're creating positive word of mouth and building your reputation indirectly, and at absolutely no cost to you (aside from your time). And you're helping the reporter by giving her the right fuel for her articles. It's a mutually beneficial situation.

Sadly, you don't provide value just by saying wacky things. Just like a reporter prepares for an interview by doing research, you need to do your part as well. This is more than simply looking up what you're being interviewed about, and it goes beyond just answering questions. If you're talking to a business reporter, read their articles, their colleagues' articles, their competitors' articles, and some broad overviews on the subject matter. Read their Twitter feed. Learn about them as a person and their beliefs. This is not Machiavellian if you're doing it so that you're more useful and interesting to them. It's basic respect, actually; you're showing you care enough that you want to do an interview with them that won't bore them or their audience to tears.

This may even mean mentioning your competitors or your peers. Why would you do that? Because you'll be telling them more than simply how great you are (in fact, use as few objective words like "great" as possible)—you're establishing context for the audience in terms of how you, as a new entrant, fit into the world. You're associating yourself with your established and respected rivals, giving them a nod of respect while also establishing that you're ready to compete in the same space. My clients don't commonly like to talk about their competition; this isn't a bad idea, but if you can give your competitors a genuine compliment while still saying you're better, that's a skill.

Humility Is the Most Attractive Trait

You've probably seen famous entrepreneurs like Elon Musk and Mark Zuckerberg make boastful comments and get tons of media attention for doing so. After co-founding PayPal, Musk created an independent luxury car company that's purely electric and an entire network of fast-charging plugs across the country. The result is that he has every license to be arrogant; he's done something incredible and created one of the most attractive, easy-to-drive, and user-friendly vehicles of all time. He has also nearly failed with both Tesla and SpaceX.

And face it—you're not Elon Musk. Unless you've created an actual perpetual-energy machine or found a way to power a phone for six days, you're not changing as much of the world as you think.

Even when those who change the world get away with bombastic, ridiculous statements, do you think most people actually want to interact with someone like that? Or rather, do people deal with boastful, brash, grandstanding types because it's good business sense to pitch them or get them onboard with an idea?

Now, don't get me wrong. If you're an entrepreneur, you're probably not the most humble person. You can't be, if you want to approach total strangers for money to invest in your idea. But you'll need to cultivate a sense of humility, and an authentic one at that.

When I was a kid, I was a deadly combination: 270 pounds and a failing student. I got beaten up and insulted on a daily basis. Teachers called me stupid. This is not an exaggeration. Psychological trauma aside, I learned humility through the rough fire of never being told I was good enough. Even when I got A's, I was told it was a fluke. Talk about negative reinforcement.

While I can't say I don't remain bitter about how I was treated, I never developed a sense of arrogance about my looks or achievements. I worked hard to change those things. More importantly, though, I learned that I could and should succeed despite constant messages that fat, dumb kids don't usually go anywhere in life. (Which is, of course, not true.)

To some, humility may not come easily. You're smart. You're an expert in your field, if not the very best in it. You know what it's like to sleep under your desk, to eat instant noodles three times a day, to have maxed-out credit cards and past-due rent, to face the constant ridicule of your friends and family members, and to experience all kinds of rejection, from business partners to vendors to romantic partners who got fed up of never seeing you. Finally, you're about to make your first media appearance. You've made it, and you want everyone to know it—especially people who were mean to you in high school. But here's the thing: if you don't get your ego in check and you instead act like a jerk, your first media appearance could very well be your last.

Also, don't forget that death is certain. No matter how much money you have, it won't follow you to the next life.

Talking Down to People Is Low

In most cases, journalists are overworked and underpaid. They tend to be very passionate about what they do and take their job seriously. You have to be fueled by passion when the hours are long, the pay is subpar, and you're intelligent enough to take a complex subject, quickly understand it, and make it digestible for the general public. Furthermore, if you're a publicist of any kind (or even a middling CEO at a semi-respectable startup), you are probably making more money and have better job prospects than most reporters you meet.

So with that in mind, here is your first rule of media relations: Do not, at any point, be condescending to a reporter. This means that when you don't know whether a reporter knows something (which you ideally have done your best to verify beforehand), ask if he knows about it in a way that's simple and conversational: "Are you familiar with [insert subject/person/place/thing here]?"

If he gets annoyed with you for asking, say, "I'm really sorry. I just want to make sure that anything I say about [subject/person/place/thing] makes sense." If he's a prick to you about that, then unfortunately, you can't do anything about it. It's probably something deeper than him just having a bad day.

If a reporter clearly hasn't done his homework, don't get upset. Ideally, he'll prepare for the interview just as much as you have, but again, these are busy, busy people. Frankly, most are doing you a favor by considering writing about your client.

One time, I had a reporter ask my client, point blank, "So, uhh . . . what are we talking about?" If I hadn't been a journalist in a previous life, I probably would've lost it, and I was surprised my client didn't.

But here's the thing: I know that we're all busy, and some interviews may seem like a waste of a client's time, but we all have to remember that much of a reporter's job is making a complex thing intelligible for readers—another set of busy people who have no idea at all about the subject. You might be an expert on a subject by virtue of it being your life's work, but reporters have to quickly learn a subject on a fairly advanced level and then distill it down into something that can be read at a seventh-grade level. (I'm not joking. A "good" newspaper article is written for someone who can read as well as a junior high student. Most are written below that standard.) Some reporters have to write and publish three to eight articles a day. If you're speaking to someone pulled in that many different directions, expect something to fall through the cracks.

Just remember: This doesn't mean writers are stupid, lazy, or dumb. If you begin thinking like that, you deserve to fail.

A very good rule of thumb is also to talk to anyone, especially on the phone, as if they were a bored 16-year-old. If they're excited, great! You will have a more pleasant and receptive interviewer, but you should still avoid putting them on the jargon bus all the way to superlative town. In fact, if you can describe what you're working on in plain language, then you're doing very well, both with the media and in understanding your own business or professional role. Journalists tend to be averse to jargon, excessive superlatives, and other linguistic bullshit. Journalism school and having their work edited by prickly, abrasive editors has made them intolerant to buzzwords. They will think you're full of shit if you're anything but plainspoken. If you insist on trying to sound smart, prepare for an onslaught of questions asking you to distill things further. This is to make it easier for their readers to grasp, not because they're mentally defective.

Your Guide to Different Kinds of Interviews

1. Phone Calls

A phone interview will usually be recorded, transcribed, and then either used as a direct question-and-answer session or, more often, used as quotes for an editorial piece that is written around the quotes. As a result, you have more freedom to talk and don't have to worry about being perfect. However, you should worry about keeping the interest of the interviewer. You have not, at this point, nailed the coverage. You have not brought it home or guaranteed anything until the ink has dried (or someone has hit the Publish button on a website back end). On a "phoner," you have one objective: to engage someone enough so that they care about writing and publishing the piece. However, do consider that there may be rare occasions when, yes, you are quoted verbatim, hesitations and all.

If you're being interviewed on the phone, try to find out beforehand how long you'll have on the phone with the reporter. Assume that most of the time, you'll have from 15 to 20 minutes, and be ready to answer the questions and deliver the most interesting information in the shortest possible time.

When you answer the phone, gauge whether the reporter is someone who likes to chitchat or someone who wants to get straight to the point. It will totally depend on the person, and picking the best route is the best way to build rapport with them. I advise, too, doing some brief searching about them beyond your basic research, like seeing on LinkedIn if they went to a similar college or worked somewhere you did. If they want to chitchat, that's an opportunity to break the ice.

I recommend keeping a one-page fact sheet that has answers to some of the more basic details, figures, talking points, and timelines on whatever it is you're being interviewed about. That way, you won't get confused or stumble on an answer, and your competency in answering the basic questions means that they'll be answered and out of the way faster.

Keep each answer to at most three sentences, unless the reporter asks you to elaborate. You want to deliver tightly honed talking points in an efficient manner. The fewer words you use, the better. Don't be terse or curt, but be straightforward with the facts. This is where your research will come in handy. You can tailor your answers to fit what the reporter is looking for, in terms of what they cover and what they're interested in, which will really make them think of you as an interesting person worth talking to.

If you can't answer a question, because of a lack of knowledge, confidentiality agreements, or any other reason, be honest. They'll respect you for it, and it's better than pissing them off with bullshit answers or being seen as a bumbling fraud. Show that you understand the world and where your product or service fits into it, rather than just being boastful and coming off as a know-it-all.

Avoid irrelevant tangents. If you can make a tangent relevant to the overall industry, go with it in order to show the reporter you know something. If it's about your life philosophy or some charming anecdote, then it's probably unnecessary. There's a big difference between rambling incoherently about a dog you saw on the street and giving a cogent opinion on something relevant that gives depth to the article.

What's really important is to make sure you actually answer a bloody question. If someone asks you something directly, you need to answer it as directly as possible. If you can't give a concrete answer, say, "We haven't set a firm [date/time/target] yet, but it'll happen in the next few weeks." This tends to work best if it's a true answer. If you don't release it in the next few weeks, or meet whatever goal you stated in the interview, follow up with them to explain, "Hey, look, this happened, and thus it's delayed." This will mean the reporter can update their story if they choose to do so. At a minimum, they know you're an honest person.

By their very nature, reporters ask difficult questions. On the phone, they don't have an audience to impress, so don't take it personally if they dig too deep. They're not grandstanding; they're just trying to get information. If they want to know about a sensitive topic (something financial or related to an upcoming development you don't want to discuss), just tell them that you can't comment.

Nothing more. Don't talk around the question. Tell them that you can't discuss it at this point, but when you're ready to talk about it, you'll keep them in the loop.

Needless to say, if you're someone who isn't great at thinking on your feet—and that's fine, not everyone is—a phone interview is a great way to get some media attention while playing to your strengths, such as delivering thoughtful, intelligent answers without feeling pressured to have perfect poise. Thankfully, lots of journalists like phone calls for similar reasons.

2. Radio

With radio, there's an even chance you'll be recorded and an even chance you'll be broadcast live. But in either case, you need to exercise more control and preparation than with the phone. You'll have much less time, sometimes as little as 60 seconds, to get your point across. The most famous people will get half an hour. That's a lifetime in any broadcast medium. Count on a few minutes if you or your product is particularly interesting.

There's a chance that you could be doing the whole thing over the phone. If it's a recorded broadcast, then hopefully you'll be invited into a studio where there are professional audio engineers and high-quality recording equipment. You'll be there with the host (the person interviewing you) and the producer, who is running the show and trying to get the best program possible. You will likely do a sound check with the microphone to make sure you sound OK, but time constraints could make that impossible. That's OK. Just sit a few inches away from the mic, clear your throat, and talk to the host as if you were in conversation with them. Speak clearly, look them in the eye, and sneak a peek at your notes if you brought any.

Sidenote: Don't Fart on the Radio

To be a dynamic, engaging, and effective radio guest, you want to eliminate as many "verbal farts" as possible. These are the "umms," "uhhs," "likes," and other verbal placeholders that we use in everyday conversation when we are hesitating in order to think of something to say. They don't sound great when speaking to someone face to face, and they make you sound like a complete imbecile on a radio show.

So what do you do if you need a split second to think of something but don't want to let out a verbal fart? Pause. I know how weird it might seem, but pausing has an effect aside from eliminating the annoying habit of saying "basically" or "kinda" or whatever placeholder happens to spew out—it lends a dramatic touch to the way you speak and gives weight to your words. You'll want to practice this habit in everyday conversation, since, if clumsily done, it could make you sound stilted and awkward in a radio broadcast. The plus side is that eliminating verbal tics from your speech patterns will improve every area of your life, not just how good you sound in an interview.

Since your time is so limited, it's important to be economical with your words. Keep each individual thought or point to one sentence. Answers should be one or two sentences long, and stories should be three or four sentences. If you think it might be OK to keep going longer, qualify this based on the host's reaction to you. If she's nodding emphatically and smiling, or otherwise showing signs that you are still interesting, then by all means, continue.

I heartily advise listening to the show in advance, as well as a few other talk-radio shows or relevant shows, and see what *you* find interesting. If you find someone boring, analyze why. Take that advice into the interview with you.

Don't stretch yourself to answer questions you can't. Stick with what you know. For example, if you're a mobile security company talking about a bank breach that happened because of a hack, and you know what happened, explain what happened. You may also want to add context, such as lax security protocols in your field or why these types of incidents matter to the wider world. But don't attempt to tie what you do to an irrelevant news story or world event.

The truth is that you could get asked anything. If you can't answer a question, you should be smart enough to talk your way out of it. If you're not, then stick to pre-recorded segments. You're not ready for the gladiator arena that is live radio.

3. Television

Television spots are much, much shorter than radio. A TV spot can be two minutes, of which you'll be talking for two 30-second chunks in between the host's two 30-second chunks. It also feels like it goes by in about 12 seconds. You'll be there for 30 to 60 minutes and only do two minutes of real work. The cameras, lights, directors, and crew-members milling about can make it nerve-racking. You'll probably be nervous, knowing that millions of people are going to see your face on live television. For these reasons, a few seconds of TV time can feel like hours in real time.

Most likely, you'll be mic'ed up by a producer. From that moment forward, do not say anything that could make you look bad when the mic is on, even if you're in the green room with four other people talking. If you have a mic on you, consider it "hot," meaning that someone in the control booth is listening or, worse, that it is already transmitting whatever you're saying. Open-mic gaffes happen all the time, and those mistakes can really fuck up how an audience perceives you or your company—including all the people who weren't tuning in but caught the embarrassing clip on late-night shows that exist to mock this sort of accident.

Listen to the producer. If she has advice, take it. If you have questions, ask them. If you are told to go into makeup, don't be offended. Each studio has different lighting, personnel, and angles, and they'll make you look your best within those parameters. The makeup is not cosmetic but rather to help you fit into the particular requirements for recording the show based on the lighting and set. Assume the best. It's in the crew's best interests to make you look good and feel comfortable. If you're a surly, uncomfortable guest, it will probably make them look bad as well.

If you are in the studio where the show is produced, to go on air, you'll walk into a room and most likely sit opposite the host. If you're on a panel of guests, you'll sit next to them. Before the cameras roll, you'll chitchat with the host or the other guests. It's a good time to get comfortable and feel at ease with the other people in the room.

In these situations, always look at the host and never at the camera. If you're on a morning show or a more conversational segment, you'll possibly be on a couch facing the hosts. Talk to them. Always. Pretend the audience does not exist.

If you are interviewed via a studio, then the whole thing is flipped. You'll see the host and other guests onscreen, but you'll want to keep looking at the camera, since you're now a proverbial "talking head." From a production standpoint, you are "facing the audience," so looking at the camera, not the host, is the correct move. When you watch your interview later, you'll see a delay of a second or so between the host asking the question and you answering. Whatever you do, don't feel bad about this when you watch it. You don't look stupid. This is how it works. It's simply a consequence of the question being transmitted over the air, and you probably wouldn't notice it if I hadn't just pointed it out.

Don't Worry, You'll Be Fine

Despite what you might cynically think, the presenters and producers are there to help you out, not trip you up. If you stumble over a sentence, do not start over. Keep going and just assume that the audience will forget your misstep two seconds later. (They actually will.) Forge ahead, keep it short and sweet, and don't forget to pause instead of making those "verbal farts." Smile, even if it's hard to. Stay positive, and be happy and grateful that you're on television.

As a TV show guest talking about some topic, you will only be talking about it. Your only goal is to be the best-sounding and most interesting person there. Talk one sentence and one thought at a time, and make sure those thoughts are actually worth hearing. If you're just there to sound smart, you're an idiot and wasting everyone's time. If you're there to be useful and be an actual source, which is your overall goal in any situation like this, then you need to actually do so.

If you are the subject of the interview (that is, the interview is about *you* and not whatever you are trying to promote), it's a lot easier to ramble, so it is crucial to remember to stick to two or three sentences per answer. Keep it as conversational and relaxed as possible, even if you're feeling nervous or uneasy. Smile at, and speak directly to, the host. Pretend there are no cameras and no other people, just the host, and you're having a drink at a bar. In most cases, this is a great choice, even on a business show, unless it's a very serious interview

155

where you're being grilled about something controversial. But don't worry, we'll cover that later.

The good news is that most TV is not that challenging. Television, including serious shows on business or political networks, is meant to entertain and inform. If you can be an entertaining, informative guest, then the producers will probably invite you back.

How to Avoid Torturing Words

It doesn't matter whether you're a corporate executive, a rock musician, or some guy making bamboo baskets in a garage in Topeka—you should be speaking to everyone as a peer. You need to remove any and all buzzwords from your vocabulary. Buzzwords are different from industry jargon, which occasionally has its place.

Buzzwords are meaningless terms that people use to make themselves seem impressive and cool. For example, on multiple, alarming occasions, I have encountered someone sincerely using the term "automagical," which means something so unbelievably automatic that it is simply magical. The people saying it were attempting to sound not just forward-thinking but, dare I say it, like a magician. What they actually sounded like was huge idiots talking about nothing.

Buzzwords are just that: buzz. Background noise. Useless. They get in the way of actual communication, and they are a great way to make a journalist think less of you. You want to reduce your signal-to-noise ratio as much as possible by focusing on the essentials in a clear, accessible way.

Your overall goal is to be understood and seen in the most positive light possible. You may speak differently depending on whether you're on a date, chatting with your parents, making small talk with someone in an elevator, or discussing your taxes with your accountant, but in all of those scenarios, you talk like a normal human being and not some self-important sociopathic automaton. It's no different when you're talking to a member of the media.

What about jargon? The main difference between jargon and buzzwords is that jargon is obscure but necessary. Every industry or field has its own jargon for a reason: you can't really describe a specific thing or situation without using those words. If you're in a highly technical field, you will probably need to use some jargon during the course of a discussion with the media. You should explain the definition to make it easier on the reporter. If a journalist isn't familiar with a term, she'll ask you to elaborate. If she knows what it means, she'll tell you. Don't take it personally either way. You're trying to communicate effectively, not to sound smart, and her job is to understand what you're saying, not to bring you down a peg. And most good reporters who cover a particular subject or beat will be familiar with the jargon already.

Before I crossed over to the dark side of PR, I was a journalist. Combine that with a generally curmudgeonly disposition, and I've become a real stickler for the English language and what things people generally hate to hear. Unfortunately, the language of Shakespeare and Faulkner and Updike has been butchered into something resembling a psychology textbook or a cruel satire of a tech-startup pitch. I've assembled a list of words and phrases that you shouldn't use, because people think they sound smart when they utter them but only end up looking and sounding like a brat.

- **That's a great question.** Well, of course, it is; that's why you're being asked it. It comes off as condescending to the reporter, and you look like you're buying time and trying to flatter them all in one go.

▶ **I can't comment on that.** Instead try, "I'm not able to go into full detail about that at the moment, but when I can, I will." If they push, just say, "I really can't—I'm sorry." They may frown at you, but it's better than saying "No comment," one of the most abrasive and useless phrases in history.

▶ **This speaks to . . .** For some reason, people use this phrase when trying to link one idea to another. There are countless other words you can use: shows, displays, demonstrates. Pick one.

▶ **We don't have any competition.** This is completely untrue in most cases, but even if you don't, try to make a comparison to something. Talk about what you fear or what could damage you. Be honest. If you do have competitors, *by all means name them.* At the very least say that there are competitors doing X, Y, and Z but that you do X, Y, and Z better, and here's why.

▶ **Our community.** Nowadays, every interest group, no matter how big or small, is a "community." A community is actually a bunch of people who live in a certain location or who are bound by some ethnic, religious, or cultural tie. Stop trying to make your platform sound like some great equalizer.

▶ **I'm really humbled.** Ever catch an award recipient saying that he is "humbled to accept this award?" What he really means is grateful, thankful, and appreciative. To be humbled means to have someone take you down a peg. Are you humbled to be appearing on a TV segment, or are you grateful that the network is having you as a guest?

- **Artisanal** and **gourmet.** I know, I know, your stuff is made by cool hipsters in a loft in Brooklyn, not some far-flung factory churning it out with cheap child labor. That does not make your product artisanal or gourmet, just overpriced and cloying. See also: "housemade" as a descriptor for something you made in your restaurant's onsite kitchen.

- **Empowering.** Sorry, but nothing consumers can purchase will ever give them a feeling of empowerment, unless they are profoundly damaged psychologically. Or it's an Iron Man suit or a way for them to recover from a debilitating injury. Don't claim that your product empowers people or that you empower your employees. You'll sound self-serving and also sort of tone-deaf.

The Narrative Fallacy

Something remarkable happens when people with good ideas or good products get the chance to sit down in front of the media and promote themselves. They screw up. I'm not talking about nerves, anxiety, or flubbing the interview, either. Yes, lots of people do that, but it's not the worst thing.

There's just something about being featured in the press that makes people turn into self-important buffoons. People who do this tend to think that a media appearance is their shot at 15 minutes of fame. Even if it technically is, they treat it as their chance to talk about how they're the most important, special creature on earth with the best invention yet.

159

They go on TV or the radio, sit down for the interview, and tell a story. More often than not, it's about something they did. Given a chance to get in front of an audience, they go into full-on huckster mode. They talk over the people interviewing them, and they insult competitors or, worse, claim they don't have any. Whatever they are doing or selling or making is described in superlative terms. It will disrupt whole industries! It will change the world! But most of all, it will make the person pitching it look like a smarmy jerk who will cause the audience to literally tune out.

On the other hand, think of a successful media appearance, something that made you want to investigate the person or product or service. How did they act? What did they talk about? How did they relate to the interviewer?

I stick by a few hard-and-fast rules. First and foremost, do a TV interview as if you were having a conversation that just happened to be recorded and broadcast to hundreds of millions of people. That statement shouldn't trigger your anxiety. Instead, it should make you pause and think about how you want to be seen by those people. Above charming, witty, or impressive, you should approach it as relaxed, gracious, and engaged. It's a bit like a job interview, except that the other person is there to make you look good rather than to qualify you as somebody worthy. Remember that you already passed the test to get on the air.

Given that we live in an era in which hype and bullshit are the primary methods of communication, one of the most powerful strategies you can employ is to give factual, concrete examples of how helpful and reliable you are or your product is.

Most people have heard the same pitches over and over, to the point where it's a cliché. When HBO has a show mocking Silicon

Valley, you know that things have gotten to a critical mass. If you are unable to find anything substantial and factual to discuss, then you may need a deeper re-think of what you are actually doing.

On Being a Human Being

I may be a consummate PR professional, but I am also, as they say in my home country, a cheeky bugger. I like stirring shit up on occasion, and in 2015, I decided that for the Consumer Electronics Show (CES), I would prank the awful PR people. You see, when you sign up for a conference as a reporter—which I did for CES, specifically and ironically to cover how PR people acted there—you're added to a gargantuan media list. The media list contains contact information for every single reporter attending. There may be an opt-out button, but I don't remember it.

I received streams of emails from PR people—obviously spammed uber-pitches of technobabble—begging me to meet with them at CES. I responded to each one by simply asking if it had updog integration. When someone asked, "What's updog?" I responded, "Nothing much, what's up with you?"

Twenty-two separate PR people fell for this trick. Each time it happened, I removed their names and posted the exchange on Twitter. It took off in a strangely viral manner.

It was a juvenile, silly prank, but the broader intent was to comment on the state of PR and tech, and how there is a never-ending race to the bottom when it comes to describing startups in hyperbolic terms. The emperor's new clothes were, to each PR person, this mythical "updog," a startup they had never heard of but that they weren't human enough to either Google or, if they knew about the joke, *not walk directly into*. Many were angry. Many were angry, in particular, that I was "wasting their time," even though they were guilty of wasting countless reporters' time and filling their inboxes with crap.

After pissing off more than my share of PR people, I got a call from a reporter about it. The journalist happened to be from a major national publication. We discussed the whole "updog" prank, but we also got to talking about other things, like my background, my path to a career in PR, and topics I don't usually touch on, like the fact that I had a learning disability as a kid but managed to overcome it, that I had started my own PR firm after moving to America and then moving to the other side of the country—basically the things you'd discuss with someone you were getting to know on a genuine level. It also helped that I had done my research and knew what he'd be interested in hearing and what would bore the shit out of him. I also talked negatively (that's an understatement) about the PR industry and some of my competitors. I know that that's generally seen as tacky. But the difference is that rather than just talk smack, I could at least cite concrete examples of how they went wrong and why—namely, that they were putting their own interests ahead of their clients. I also did not use any buzzwords or other annoying language.

The result was that a conversation that could have been negative, resulting in bad press, was a positive one. I established a relationship with a prominent journalist, and we ended up relating on a very human level. Reporters and their readers are people, too. If you can come across that way, it will go a long way toward enhancing the way you are viewed—especially when you need to say things that are uncomfortable. If you say them with conviction rather than malice, then you will be taken seriously. But it doesn't always go that smoothly.

Take Stewart Butterfield, the CEO of Slack, a business chat solution that's become huge and gotten fantastic press, partially on the back of Stewart's amenable, chatty attitude and willingness to be blunt and entertaining.

In an interview with *Wired* (http://www.wired.com/2014/08/the-most-fascinating-profile-youll-ever-read-about-a-guy-and-his-boring-startup/), it's clear how Butterfield has managed to rally a number of supporters behind his growing (and kinda difficult to understand) communications platform. The child of draft-dodging hippies, he grew up on a commune in Canada and was originally named Dharma, which he's happy to joke about in interviews. After he sold his first company, the photo-sharing service Flickr, to Yahoo, he wrote an amusing now-public resignation letter that endeared him to many http://www.businessinsider.com/stewart-butterfield-epic-resignation-letter-2014-8).

The media loves him because of his forthcoming attitude, which can be crude but charming. He swears in interviews and makes brutally candid comments like, "I fucking hate Valleywag." He is honest about the product he has built and doesn't obfuscate the truth with buzzwords or other sleight-of-hand tricks infamous in the world of tech startups. He is ambitious but still humble. It's an award-winning combo that feeds directly into the public image of the growing company he runs.

When an Interview Is Going South

An interview going badly is practically a rite of passage both for journalists and for people in the hot seat. You can prepare all you want, be on your best behavior, and do everything I tell you to do, but at some point, it will happen.

It's important to classify exactly how an interview is going poorly.

There're two different ways to tell if an interview is going wrong, and they mostly happen on the phone:

1. You're a shitty subject. This is self-explanatory. It could be that you are boring, said something that rubbed a reporter the wrong way, or are making their job harder. It could very well be something that you didn't even notice. At the very least, you can turn things around if you understand it.

2. You have a hostile reporter. This is entirely possible, and big companies will have PR staff who are trained to intervene and prevent them from getting even remotely ugly. Since you're reading this book, you don't have that luxury.

Before You React, Respond

When your interview is going to shit, then your first reaction will be, well, a reaction. You might feel a bit of anxiety or panic as you realize that this is not going according to plan at all. But you don't need to lose it.

First of all, stop and determine the reason for the hostility or boredom that the reporter is displaying. The first thing you need to do is take a mental assessment of what is going on.

A conversation can go sideways for any number of reasons that have nothing to do with you. Someone might be having a bad day, they may be rushed, or they may have forgotten about the call. They might be put out because their spouse was short with them before they left for work or because their dog is sick.

Do not use this line of thinking as a crutch to absolve yourself of any responsibility, but you and I both know we've lost our cool with people who didn't deserve it, merely on account of factors making us grouchy before the day even got started.

If the reporter does mention something like that, there's nothing wrong with saying, "Hey, look, if you want to reschedule, I totally understand." If they say not to worry about it, which in my history has always been the case, there's nothing to do but move forward knowing the person is going to be a little downbeat. They probably want to keep going to make sure their mind stays off whatever is bothering them and as a point of pride. The ideal situation is that they agree to reschedule, but I find that this rarely happens.

If it's not some external factor setting them off, then you need to think about what, if anything, you did and try to correct it.

Do not be confrontational. If you ask, "Am I boring you?" then you'll come off as a petulant jerk, and their suspicions about you will be confirmed right off the bat.

On the other hand, a bit of self-deprecation works wonders. Saying something like "I get the sense you're not as thrilled by what I'm talking about as I am" not only pokes fun at you but gives them an out to explain themselves in a non-confrontational manner. You're not dealing with an evil tyrant dictator here. Giving the other person an opportunity to avoid feeling rude or confrontational is a very powerful tool in these situations. The feedback you'll hear is also valuable, objective criticism from an honest third party. Most reporters don't want to hurt your feelings and aren't used to having someone deal with them on an honest and outgoing level. There may be some who jerk you around and are mean. There will be more who appreciate the honest question.

Permission to Treat the Witness as Hostile

If you've ever watched a courtroom drama, you've probably seen an episode where one of the lawyers asks the judge for "permission to treat the witness as hostile." The judge almost always agrees, and the lawyer rips into the witness and saves the day for their client right before commercial break.

Unless you've gone out of your way to be obstinate and difficult, a reporter won't tend to want to treat you as hostile. Provocations are one thing, and typically, aggressive questioning is the mark of arrogant amateurs trying to make a name for themselves. Thankfully, these types of reporters are few and far between. If a reporter's line of questioning is in bad faith *and* wrong, then by all means, go ahead and challenge him. You can treat him as hostile if this happens. If his facts are incorrect, politely but firmly correct them. Challenge any assertions he makes, where they are coming from, who said them, and whether he tried to verify them. Beyond preparation, facts and quotes are sacrosanct to any good journalist. Make sure he has his right before he tries to use them against you. And no matter how flustered you get, you'll still want to kill him with kindness. Playing nice will disarm him and challenge any prejudice he seems to have toward you, and if he still doesn't let up, it will make him look like a real low-life if he persists in antagonizing you.

Most journalists really do want to get the story, get it right, and be nice to you so that if they ever need to speak to you again, you'll pick up the phone. But it's important to know how to spot the bad apples. Also, death is certain, and one bad interview won't ruin your life.

The Give and Take Between You and a Reporter

Most relationships, whether platonic, professional, or even romantic, are based on some sort of exchange. In a lot of situations, you might ask yourself, "What does the other person bring to the table, and what can they do for me?" Framed the wrong way, this seems like an extraordinarily callous thing to say, especially when it comes to people you love. But you should look at it in the context of reciprocity. Someone is capable of doing something for you, and the right thing to do is to return the favor once in a while.

This is the key to understanding and maintaining great relationships with those in the media. In addition to needing access to your client, some reporters will want background information. Reporters may ask you for data or documents that will require you to use your discretion. If the bit of information that they want is something that you *can* share but is not in the public domain, then you've just handed them something really useful, and they're not likely to forget it.

But enough about what you can do for an ink-stained wretch. You want to know what some lousy journalist can do to help you. Well, that depends. If you don't make time for them, you can't expect much in return.

If you've taken the time to cultivate a relationship, answered their questions, or briefed them on topics they didn't understand, then the door to a reciprocal relationship has been opened. What does that mean for you? Well, how about introductions to other reporters and more coverage of you or whatever your business is doing? You won't necessarily get favorable coverage for helping a reporter, but cultivating a reciprocal relationship certainly won't hurt your chances.

Department of Corrections

Every reporter makes errors, and sometimes the fact checkers don't catch every mistake. It happens. Open a major paper on any given day, and you'll see at least one correction. Some newspapers keep track the old-fashioned way, and if a reporter makes too many mistakes, they get axed. Believe me when I say reporters have every incentive to get every fact correct.

Although quotes are considered the cornerstone of reporting, people have been misquoted before, including me, and they will continue to be misquoted as long as journalism exists. The move from writing stuff down to digital voice recorders has undoubtedly helped, but it hasn't eliminated errors.

If you're misquoted, before you flip out on the reporter or contact their editor, you should make sure that you actually didn't say whatever you think came across poorly. This may sound silly, but people can have selective memory. Many reporters deal with sources who are unhappy after the fact not because of factual errors but simply because they no longer like how they phrased an answer or presented their ideas. You may not like the way things sound now that you've seen it printed. If you didn't specify that something was "on background" or "off the record," then the reporter had the right to print it, and you're out of luck. If you did specify that, you have proof in writing or on your own recording, and the reporter printed it anyway, then by all means contact their editors. They will be displeased with the ethics violation their reporter committed.

If there was a factual error on your part, then it is absolutely your responsibility to inform the reporter of it. If the processor in your mobile device is 3.1 GHz and they quoted it as 3.2 GHz, then it's not a huge deal, but it ought to be corrected. For something bigger, like a 25 percent difference in the device's battery life versus what it is really capable of, you absolutely want to rectify it because it's a major error about your product.

It's a case of a cost-benefit analysis of potentially embarrassing someone. Everyone makes typos, and I don't think anyone is happy to hear that they made them. Some people, especially those who make money selling their words, might be quite embarrassed when they make a mistake. Things like grammar or spelling errors (unless it's your name) don't need to be brought to their attention. Often, those sorts of mistakes are due to multiple editors fussing with the same story before it goes to print.

If the journalist did make an error regarding something factual or otherwise important to your livelihood, then you are right to ask for a correction. The first step is to contact them privately, let them know that they reported something incorrectly, and see if they can change it. As always, if you're polite and gracious, you'll be more likely to get the desired results.

If you don't get a response after several attempts, then it's time to escalate. You may not be able to find out exactly who their editor or producer or manager is, but you can probably find some contact information for the outlet, including whatever department oversees editorial. You can call or email them and explain that your attempts to get the error remedied have been unsuccessful. Again, this needs to be something that really warrants a correction, because the next steps involve contacting the editor-in-chief and harassing the reporter's bosses to get something removed. Doing this will sink your chances of getting future coverage from them.

When You've Sprung a Leak

Here's the problem with leaks. You can't do much about them. If an employee or someone close to your organization leaks confidential information to the media, then you have an internal crisis bigger than your run-of-the-mill PR problem.

Not too long ago, a well-known blog scooped major outlets on a story regarding a major American company having delays with a key new product. The source for the story was an employee on the engineering side, though the issue involved the company's inability to work with an important new material. The material supplier ended up issuing a statement that didn't deny that the problem existed but merely stated that the problem was not a result of their material. The company stayed silent on the matter. It later emerged that the problems were indeed real, but the matter was divulged in an investment bank's equity research report rather than in an official PR statement. One company got in front of the story, while the other hid from it.

So who handled it well, and who dropped the ball? Well, it's hard to say. The supplier's stock price took a bit of a hit because of the report, but at least they got in front of the story. The company, whose shareholders include major institutional investors, evidently had to have the problem exposed via other channels—and in that industry, an equity research report is a far more damning news source than traditional media.

The larger issue here is that it was not some rumor that was made up out of thin air. The spread of accurate-but-confidential information can damage your reputation or your bottom line. You might be able to deny it, but more than likely it will come back to bite you. A simple, curt "We're looking into it" will also suffice, but do your best not to come off like you're hiding something, and truly try to find out what happened. And, of course, if you are friendly with the reporter, say, "I promise you we'll get back to you the moment we understand the entire situation."

If the leak in question is incorrect and can be verified as false, you're playing a different game. This is also a rare occurrence, but it has happened. You should, as contentious as this can be, escalate the problem immediately by talking to the editor-in-chief and showing evidence to the contrary. Keep the exchange as positive and unthreatening as you can. For example, if a publication claims that your company is out of, or not making any, money, presenting the editor with revenue statements or documentation signed by your Certified Public Accountant is a powerful way to neutralize those claims.

It may seem strange, because they have effectively attacked you, but you can do a lot of good here if you try to be a mediator. You'd be surprised by how well people respond when they're wrong (and especially if they are super wrong and made something up) and are not immediately flayed by a lawyer. Explain that you're not looking to cause any trouble and that all you want is a retraction (this is different than a correction). A retraction is an explicit admission that what an outlet published was incorrect.

In the event they do not do so, you may have to make a public statement of your own on your blog. Whatever you do—even now, even when somebody hasn't played ball with you—do not attack the reporter. Say "X reporting happened at Y outlet, and it's verifiably false. Here is the information that verifies that falsehood." They may update the post. They may not. There may be brand damage, and if it's significant, you may want to consider legal action. Most likely, if you are honest and up front, you will win hearts and minds.

When to Lawyer Up

In these situations, people naturally want to bring in a lawyer or some kind of legal action to remedy the situation. There is nothing wrong with getting legal advice, and that's why lawyers exist. Depending on your industry and your particular needs, you may be able to receive an hour of free legal advice from a reputable firm without having to put a legal team on retainer. Especially if you're a small company or a sole proprietor, this matters a great deal to your bottom line.

Involving a lawyer, whether it's for a cease-and-desist letter, a lawsuit, or something in between, is another matter. Your lawyer will be able to advise you on the most appropriate course of action in a given situation. By all means, follow her advice. But when you involve a lawyer, your relationship with a reporter or an outlet will change forever, almost always in a negative way. I'm not saying that's a reason to avoid legal action, but I do caution you to rely on a lawyer only as an appropriate, measured response to a threatening situation.

Lawyers are a nuclear weapon. The moment they get involved, you will cause a lot of trouble and scare the reporter. It's frightening to be threatened with legal action! You must remember that whatever you do will have a permanent effect on your relationship with the outlet and the reporter. Word will likely spread that you threatened or sued the reporter or publication. *Nobody* in the media who gets wind of this will forget it. Ever.

Unless you will suffer real, lasting harm, something irrevocably terrible and *truly not your fault*, do not bring your lawyer into it. A reporter can also say, "The company brought their lawyers in," which is the opposite of good press.

When in Doubt, Apologize

Have you ever heard somebody say, "I'm sorry you feel that way"? That's the most obnoxious, condescending way to say to somebody, "I see you're upset. I don't give a fuck." Not apologizing for your mistakes is among the vilest of human traits. But sometimes you need to suck it up. Try saying, "I'm sorry. How can I fix this?"

Reporters aren't the only ones who make mistakes. As a publicist, I have made mistakes with reporters far more often than I'd like to admit. I've sent information late. I've relayed incorrect information about the product, either because the client gave me the wrong information and I didn't fact-check or simply because I got it wrong. Being called out is an ego blow, and taking responsibility sucks. But it's a necessary part of life. Being contrite and saying, "I'm sorry—I fucked up" is always better than the ego-driven alternatives: burning a bridge, lying to weasel out of a situation, or throwing a reporter under the bus to save your skin. Not only are those unprofessional things to do, but you're letting pride stand in the way of being a decent person.

Cultivating that moral clarity should free up your emotional resources so that you can focus on making tough decisions, such as letting a client suffer the consequences of screwing up an opportunity.

Recently, I had to tell a producer of a national TV show that my client had to back out because he was scared to talk about cybersecurity in light of an Obama administration cyber-policy statement. The client had worked with the Obama administration and had been on various committees discussing technology with the President, but for some reason, when the time came, he was too spooked to comment. (He also seemed annoyed that he couldn't just promote his own product and services.)

I emailed the producer with an honest update: The client wouldn't do the show because he was too nervous to talk about cybersecurity, even though I was relatively sure that wasn't what they would be talking about on the program. The producer confirmed that what she wanted to discuss wasn't related to security, and I told her how furious I was with my uncooperative client. I explained that I had made it clear to the client that this was a mistake that would make him look bad and hurt his relationship with the producer. I mentioned again that I was absolutely furious and that the client was making a huge mistake, and that I was so sorry that any of this happened.

I handled this situation the way I did because I sincerely believe that sometimes you have to tell the truth, even if it's not the best truth and even if it means losing a client. Because I was honest, there's a good chance that the producer will invite my client back and that the relationship is actually better because she knows more about how my client behaves and what topics are off-limits. She might not have the highest opinion of my client, but at least she knows who she's dealing with.

There will always be that reporter who responds with a fiery, rude "I'm done with you forever!" It's hard to accept, but in the end, there's not much you can do. There will always be reporters who don't like you because you're being yourself, but for every one of them, 10 more will appreciate your candor. The price you pay in the short term will earn you greater respect and trust in the future.

Crisis Communications

Crisis communications is one of the most famously lucrative and also lied-about topics in the world of public relations. It really is its own specialty field, and one which I hope you'll never have to utilize.

It's important to define what counts as a "crisis" and when you need "crisis communications." Did your company cause a major environmental disaster? Is it responsible for the death of a human being?

Did someone commit a crime, or is someone guilty of fraud? If yes, then you better pick up the phone and call a professional.

If your CEO said something racist or made some kind of remark that offended a particular group, that's a conventional PR problem. Not that there's anything conventional about disparaging statements, and as we are seeing, the power of blogs and social media can quickly turn something like a disparaging remark—or one taken out of context—into a crisis for your organization.

Rule Number One: Think, Don't Act—Yet

Whatever you may think of George W. Bush, there was one instance where I felt he was unfairly portrayed as unintelligent when, in fact, he did *the best thing possible* in a time of crisis. I don't mean this politically. This isn't a politics book. I mean that I approve of what he did from a mediated, likely press-secretary-driven standpoint.

The now infamous footage of our 43rd president learning about the September 11th attacks and then sitting in silent reflection for a number of minutes has become emblematic of what many people see as a bumbling, stilted response to a world-changing event.

People who hold this idea are, in my opinion, total fucking morons who have never had to deal with anything bigger than their local bakery being sold out of cronuts. When something goes wrong, I want you to think, "What Would Dubya Do?"

Note that this does not excuse you from taking action. But it also neutralizes a far-more-dangerous impulse, which is to act out of rash emotion. Avoid doing that at all costs. It's the PR equivalent of drunk-dialing an ex.

When faced with news of a bad situation, stop and take a few minutes to calm yourself and absorb the gravity of the situation. If

George W. Bush can do that and then get to work on responding to the first domestic act of war since Pearl Harbor, then you can and should be able to pivot to acting on the situation right away.

Establish the Facts

What are the facts of a situation? This may seem like the dumbest question in the world, but it's important. When things are really going poorly, your mind will be spinning in a million different directions. You need to establish the core problem and the peripheral details. This will help you clearly define your issue, as well as where and when it happened, who was involved, and any other pertinent details that you need to tackle.

If you have a staff or a team working with you, this is even more important. If you can establish a definitive timeline with dates, names, locations, and other details, it will save you from having to explain the situation over and over again and offer a consistent record of what happened. That can be an additional challenge in a crisis, and one you should avoid if possible. Just make sure that your internal documentation is housed in some kind of secure, internal system that can be accessed by *only* the people who should be reading it. The last thing you need to combat is a leak about your plan to respond before you've actually had time to do so.

Don't Even Think About Lying

This is so elementary that I shouldn't even have to mention it, but humans often overestimate their own abilities. Sometimes that means that in critical situations, where they should know better, they take the sleazy way out by lying or rationalizing to avoid making a hard decision or facing the consequences of their actions.

Lying will benefit you in the short term, but it will always, without fail, bite you in the ass down the road, and the damage will be exponential. The public has a lot of patience and compassion for people or companies that make mistakes. But they have very little tolerance for lying scumbags.

Take the National Football League (NFL), arguably the most beloved professional sports organization in the United States. Numerous NFL players have had run-ins with law enforcement, but in the past, those athletes were punished with appropriate severity. (Mostly. Sort of.)

But the recent domestic-violence scandal involving Ray Rice, a star player, brought the league to its knees. In case you missed it, video evidence surfaced that showed Rice knocking his fiancée unconscious in an elevator. When the footage was made public, the NFL disavowed all knowledge of the tapes and suspended Rice for a paltry two games.

As if the backlash over the light suspension weren't enough, a *second* video surfaced after the NFL instituted a new policy on domestic violence. The NFL denied that it had known of the video's existence, but evidence emerged that the league's internal investigation had been insufficient, casting doubt on whether the league could police itself. We may never know whether NFL officials saw the damning evidence before it went public, but if the league is ever found to be lying about its handling of the Rice scandal, it will cause even more turmoil for the league, its players, and fans of American football.

Get in Front of the Situation
My attorney, Austin So, uses the perfect crisis communication phrase: "Get in front of the situation." Unfortunately, this is often

misinterpreted as, "Make sure your message is out there before another person or social media account grabs it first."

What it actually means is that you need to take action—even if that means establishing a timeline of events—before things get worse. Often, you won't have all the information you need to appreciate the gravity of the situation. And you know what? That's OK. As long as you are doing something about it, it's perfectly reasonable to say, "Something has happened, we do not know what it is, and we see the reports out there. We are looking into it."

Remember that timeline I told you to craft in the immediate aftermath of a situation? It has an additional purpose. You will use that same information to craft your first official public statement, whether written or broadcast, giving your side of the story. This is the most important statement you'll make, as you will be held accountable to it for a long time to come. It will include:

A. What happened

B. How it happened

C. Why it happened

D. What you're going to do about it

Knowing these key facts will help you save as much face as possible. The first three items are objective matters that aren't really up for interpretation. Even if each party's supposed facts differ, if you truly believe that certain events played out in a certain way, then those will be the facts you use to confront the problem. The final item is where things get tricky.

You need to show some kind of concrete, tangible evidence that you will right the situation. In certain situations—like an executive recorded using a racial slur in private—a sincere apology, released separately from your initial statement, is mandatory. You may want to consider a charitable donation as well—either a one-time donation or an ongoing donation of profits—though you'll inevitably hear accusations that you're trying to buy your way out of the problem. You can't please everybody, but at least you'd be offering more than words as an apology.

Next up on the ladder of major crises is a high-profile business leader or executive having mental-health issues, having a substance-abuse problem, or being involved in a criminal act. In these situations, criminal charges notwithstanding, the best thing the person in question can do is take a leave of absence and deal with whatever needs to be dealt with. More than likely, they will resist—they don't want to step away from work, there's too much money at stake, and investors will lose confidence in them and perhaps the company. These are all valid concerns. But giving someone the necessary time to solve their own problems trumps any business-related concern. This response carries more weight than words, and it demonstrates to the public that serious effort to remedy the issue is underway, not some bandage solution trotted out in hopes that people will forget about it.

Product Problems

PR problems involving your product or service can seem like the end of the world. Founders and investors tend to treat these issues as if a relative were sick or dying, and I totally empathize. When you've poured that much time and money into something, it really does seem like your baby.

But it's OK. A crappy line of code or something that's poorly built isn't nearly as serious as human life. You may not see it that way, but the rest of the world recognizes that a product flaw is a small problem in an inanimate object.

Put yourself in the shoes of the founder of a promising startup. Right as you are trying to raise more funding to help your project scale, a hacker finds a major security breach in your product, one that could compromise the personal and financial information of your entire user base.

Do you:

A. Publicly announce what you've found, fix the breach, and take steps to make your product even safer?

B. Do a cost-benefit analysis and hope the problem goes away?

C. Ignore it because you really can't afford to fix it?

D. Try to sweep it under the rug so that the VC firms you are pitching keep returning your phone calls?

Obviously, A is the ideal answer, but you're not always faced with the ideal situation. Option B is what I call the "Pinto problem." Back in the 1970s, Ford knew about a potentially fatal defect in its small Pinto automobile. Rear-end crashes could cause the fuel tank to rupture and launch the car into a fiery wreck, burning the passengers alive. In a moment of unparalleled callousness, Ford decided it was cheaper to settle the lawsuits regarding the deaths or injuries that resulted than to initiate a recall. It's a wonder anyone still buys their cars anymore. But at the same time, people haven't forgotten about this, and they likely never will. Reacting in this manner is a surefire way to kill your startup and your career.

What about Option C? You are faced with a serious problem, but you're too broke or short-staffed to fix it. Theoretically, you *could* just ignore it and hope it goes away, but when someone finds out, it will be ugly. The best way to salvage things is to come totally clean: Admit that you ignored the problem because [you had financial constraints, didn't have the resources to fix it, etc.]. If nothing else, the honesty and contrition will win you points with the public. You may lose money or customers, but not as badly as if you choose Option D.

Option D is the dumb, short-term solution that always catches up with you. Option D is for the scared, weak PR professionals whose egos outweigh their abilities. Yes, having to face lost revenue and pissed-off customers after you've been honest and forthright is a crappy feeling. But it will never be as bad as if you'd lied or tried to bury the problem.

in case of emergency, break open this chapter

My vision for this book is to give the entrepreneur or employee the ability to take control of PR on their own, without experience or formal training in the field (or even a college degree). I deliberately structured the last five chapters to give you a crash course in PR. The goal of the book is right there in the title: I want you to feel comfortable enough to fire your publicist. If you're already a publicist, I want you to feel confident enough to get fired.

But I don't want to leave you hanging, either. There's a very good chance that things will go wrong at some point in your career or that you'll need to brush up on something at the last second, but that doesn't mean you need to feel like it's time to crawl into a hole and die or, worse, rush to hire the first PR "professional" you can find in the yellow pages.

My goal for this chapter is to give you a handy reference that will help you navigate some of the most common (and most dangerous) PR situations. Think about it like one of those fire extinguishers you'd see in school. Remember the ones that had the big red letters that read IN CASE OF EMERGENCY, BREAK GLASS?

And just as you don't need to know how a fire extinguisher works to put out a fire, you don't need to be a PR pro to put a stop to a bad situation. Add your own common sense to the following lessons, and you'll be able to put out fires.

Handling a Defective Product

About 40 years ago, in his book *Quality Is Free,* Philip Crosby outlined a management theory called "zero defects." The theory rapidly gained traction. Along with a mandate for defect-free products, one of its central tenets was that those involved with a project should not even think about adopting the attitude that defects are inevitable, since that would invariably cause defects. Instead, they should demand a defect-free product by keeping the heat on their suppliers to maintain quality and should rain fire and brimstone upon them if they slip up.

(http://www.amazon.com/Quality-Is-Free-Certain-Business/ dp/0070145121 Crosby PB. *Quality Is Free: The Art of Making Quality Certain.* McGraw-Hill Companies. 1979.)

But back here on planet Earth, we know that, inevitably, shit happens. It should also go without saying that the definition of *defective* is not "broken"—it's that something is imperfect, faulty, or deficient to the point that it does not do what it promises to do. If you release an app with a sucky user interface that freezes sporadically, it is not "defective"; it still works, it just sucks. If your app costs money, crashes constantly, and has a security flaw that lets hackers steal the personal information of your users, then you're in the realm of legitimately defective. If this book were 40 percent gibberish, it'd be defective. If your smartphone doesn't connect to the Internet at LTE speeds but advertises that it does, that's defective. If the core functionality of your product is incomplete or only quasi-usable, it's defective.

Part of me is amazed that people think they can still get away with releasing defective products in this day and age. For one thing, it's totally unethical. And in this era of ubiquitous media coverage of every single tiny niche, believing that you can get away with this behavior can come only from a cocktail of staggering arrogance and stupidity. In such cases, none of my advice can save you.

Talk to a Lawyer

My first piece of advice to you is quite simple: Contact a lawyer. Why? Three reasons:

1. You want the advice of someone who is intelligent and also removed from the situation. Your emotions are probably running high, and this tends to cloud your judgment. If nothing else, a lawyer's take on the situation can provide clarity.

2. You could very well be exposed to legal liability, and you need to cover your ass. This goes for software, too, not just hardware and other tangible goods.

3. Your lawyer actually knows the law and thus will know what you should not do now that you have potentially put yourself at legal risk. Lawyers have graduated from law school and passed the bar. You likely have not.

This should go without saying, but *never* say anything to anybody—not even your own employees or partners—before you speak to your lawyer. Once that's settled, you have to swallow a particularly bitter pill, which is that even if the situation is not your *fault*, it's still your *problem*.

What do I mean by that exactly?

Let's pretend that you're a kitchenware company, and you're about to launch a brand-new, state-of-the-art blender. You've done a huge marketing push on all the major daytime TV shows, landed stories in the press and the major online outlets, and managed to make people give a shit about a blender, which is no small feat.

Armed with thousands of pre-orders, you're riding high and anticipating what should be a cakewalk of a launch day, when all of a sudden you get reports of your blender being completely broken. Some of the blenders are literally broken—the glass is shattered, the plastic parts are cracked—and others don't quite work properly when they are plugged in. After a frantic investigation, you discover that the packaging supplier that you contracted to pack the blenders with Styrofoam and bubble wrap used cheap paper and little else. There is nothing wrong with your blenders, save for being too fragile to handle the logistics-company employees tossing them off the conveyor belt and onto the truck with absolutely zero care.

Not your fault, right? Don't be so sure. Your due diligence sucked. You didn't monitor your entire supply chain.

But it's still your product, your brand, and, ultimately, your problem. You can tell the whole world the story of how a third party let you down, but nobody will care, and you'll look like an asshole for throwing someone under the bus to distract from your problem. So it's time to take the high road.

Responding in a forthright, honest manner is always a good strategy. Remember when I told you to talk to your lawyer? There's another benefit to that, which is that it will give you a cooling-off period to help you gather your thoughts rather than make yet another anxiety-driven gaffe. Lawyers make excellent substitute therapists in that you can say to them all the stupid things you want to say publicly, and they will remind you, "Please do not say that publicly."

If your lawyer is any good, she'll probably be willing to help you out with an apology. Attorneys are the masters of carefully crafting words to achieve a desired outcome, and yours will probably have a good idea of how to express contrition without giving your detractors anything additional to work with. A lawyer may not craft the most emotional statement, so you will want to work with her to make sure your soul isn't lost in what will *ultimately be an apology and a promise of improvement.*

In this theoretical example, you want to let the press and the public know that you are deeply sorry, and that all the blenders will be replaced free of charge. You can privately fire the supplier and ream them out, but you'll have to find a new supplier to make sure it doesn't happen again. To make amends above and beyond what's needed, which is always a good course of action, you'll want to give your customers a gift card, an additional free product, or something substantial as a token of your gratitude for standing by your product. I know, I know. You might have crowdfunded the blender. You might not be *able to afford to do that.* That's why people have this thing called insurance built into their businesses. If you don't have that and you really messed up, the result will not be pretty but should be *honest.* Whatever you do, *do not lie to get out of a bad situation.*

This kind of customer service will be immensely costly in the short term, but the long-term payoff, in terms of reputation and publicity, is significant and could make or break your entire company. This might seem like a theme throughout the book, and it is a keystone of my philosophy. Doing the right thing might be tough to quantify—or swallow—in the midst of a crisis, but it is a sure-fire way to come out looking favorable.

When you release your statement, a firm timeline will enhance your credibility even further. Never, ever use a word like "shortly." Announce a real deadline for yourself, and make your staff stick to it. If you can't, there's nothing wrong with saying, "At this time, we don't know when we'll know more. We are very sorry." If it's going to be a while, make that clear and clearly state that you deeply regret that you can't speed up the process.

Trust is lost quickly and regained slowly. The best way to regain it is to show people that you care and that you want to fix things, tell them how you're going to do so, and then follow through on it.

If Your Product Is Just Plain Bad

Your product may not be defective, but it may not be well received by the public or the media. The reasons for this are so varied that it's not worth exploring every single one of them. And if you are who I think you are—someone who is passionate about their product, who lives and breathes what they do and takes every bit of constructive criticism as a personal assault on their character—then any dissection of why you are getting negative press will only further divert your attention from the positive aspects of a poor reception of your product.

Yes, you read that right. There are positives to this scenario, even if it's not the ideal. Think of all the bad reviews or reactions to your product as free, unbiased focus groups. I understand that there are compromises in the development of any product, whether it's a physical good or software, but that doesn't mean you can fall back on that as an excuse for not achieving your desired goals. But you can take the information and use it to improve your product for next time. And you know what? There's a silver lining here, too. People will be very interested in you and your story if you can come back with a vastly improved product that defies expectations *and* has a great PR story behind it. One of the great things about American culture is that failure is not a mark of shame. Everyone loves an underdog, and contrition is seen as a sign of character, not weakness. A comeback story that combines a truly great product and real evidence of working to correct your mistakes is the stuff of magazine covers and feature articles. But you get only one shot at it. Make it count.

On the other hand, if you can afford to delay the launch of your product to address its faults or deficiencies, then by all means, do so! In the video-game industry, new releases are frequently pushed out before they are truly ready to come to market. A combination of internal pressure from game developers and impatience from customers means that companies increasingly release titles early.

A great case study here is that of the social network Path, founded by a charming former Facebook engineer, Dave Morin. Path launched in 2010 as a tightly restricted social network with limited photo-sharing functionality. It rose and fell like a very fat dolphin, and people sort of forgot about it until the second version, which had clearly been revamped to address a lot of the initial criticism, arrived in 2011. Path engineers had raised the friend limit from 50 to 150, built a truly gorgeous interface with a quick and easy way to share photos, and added the ability to share what time you wake up, what time you go to bed, and what music you're listening to. In fact, Path 2.0 was what the original was meant to be—a personal social network—which is why influential writer and venture capitalist Om Malik called it "What Facebook Should Be" (https://gigaom.com/2011/11/30/ hands-on-with-path-2-0-what-facebook-should-be/).

Path was suddenly hot again. But a scandal was waiting in the wings. The company had promised "Path does not retain or store any of your information in any way." But that was not the case. After waves of positive press in 2011, hubris pie was served at Path HQ when hacker Arun Thampi discovered that Path was importing users' entire address books without their consent (http://blog.mclov .in/path-uploads-your-entire-iphone-address-book-to-its-servers-22HGO5EiLJKhWZPKdMOgdw).

Path was slammed by the Federal Trade Commission with an $800,000 fine for deceiving consumers and collecting personal information from minors without consent, among other things (https://www .ftc.gov/news-events/press-releases/2013/02/path-social-networking-app-settles-ftc-charges-it-deceived). In Silicon Valley, that's chump change. Path had already taken more than $40 million in venture-capital funding.

Path CEO Morin apologized. The site rebounded again. In April 2013, the *Wall Street Journal* reported that Path was adding a million new users a week. But that victory would be short-lived (http://blogs.wsj.com/digits/2013/04/25/path-a-social-diary-app-is-adding-1-million-new-users-a-week/).

A month later, Path was accused of spamming users. At the time, when users signed in to the app, they were encouraged to invite all their Facebook friends and contacts. The issue was that it wasn't abundantly clear that you were about to blast your friends via SMS or Facebook with a message to join Path. One particularly irked TechCrunch commenter noted, "Part of my job is to test apps. Lots and lots of apps. I have seen thousands of sign-up funnels. This is the first time I have seen my entire contact book contacted at once without me being able to select who." Morin blamed the issue on the growing pains that plague any small company that experiences great success. But those types of responses, although not full-blown lies, obfuscate the truth. There are ethical ways to succeed that mean you will grow at a slower rate. Path is a great example as to why it's worth planning for slow, ethical growth rather than a meteoric rise (and then a crash back to earth).

All the charm and PR offense in the world couldn't save Morin or Path. The social network's popularity continued to plummet. In early 2015, makers of the South Korean messaging app KakaoTalk acquired Path, probably to leverage Path's foothold in Indonesia.

Path's fall from grace in America can certainly be attributed to a disjointed product that never quite hit home and a company flailing for relevance in the face of WhatsApp, Facebook, and even Google+. But for a long time Path had the hearts and minds of millions, even after its initial problems. However, they bet incorrectly on user growth and hoped that Morin's charm and résumé would be enough to withstand any backlash. Customers never forget when they've been tricked, and most demand contrite apologies, even if they never return to a service. A bad product, even with heaps of positive publicity, can withstand only so much.

Gaming: Where Some People Move Fast and Break Hearts

Video games are odd products in that game-company executives often try to satisfy the demand for new games by pushing a title out the door before it's been checked for bugs, gameplay issues, and other technical problems. It's an incredibly shortsighted line of thinking. Many businesspeople seem to prefer it, but it's never worth it in the long term.

Ubisoft, a noted game developer, did exactly this when it released *Assassin's Creed: Unity*, which is part of a major game franchise that has sold tens of millions of copies and that I used to quite like. Because of the massive anticipation for *Unity*, and under pressure from stockholders with an unquenchable thirst for profits, Ubisoft released the game early. It had issues before it even launched. Ubisoft had canceled plans to include female playable characters in the game's multiplayer mode [http://kotaku.com/ubisoft-cut-plans-for-female-assassins-in-unity-1589278349]. Their reasoning was that it would be too expensive to do so, citing the cost of motion capture and voice actors.

The public was naturally furious. People tore *Unity* apart before it was even released, and Ubisoft received a huge black eye for a series that had otherwise been a shining star in their portfolio. Their response was inadequate, simply saying that they had diversity in their titles and that they wanted to highlight the story of Arno, the game's protagonist [http://kotaku.com/ubisoft-responds-to-assassins-creed-female-character-co-1589413130]. A smart move would have been to spend some of the game's massive marketing budget on adding a female character. This would also have been an excellent excuse to delay the game and fix technical problems that should have been solved before the game shipped.

Ubisoft also hadn't been forthcoming with early review copies [http://www.polygon.com/2014/11/11/7193415/assassins-creed-unity-review-embargo]. This was a bad sign. Above and beyond its technical issues, even creative elements like the plot were criticized as poorly thought out. The reaction was so negative that Ubisoft offered free game titles and downloadable content [http://www.pcgamer.com/assassins-creed-unity-free-game-offer-is-now-underway/].

Ubisoft did the right thing when it came to treating their customers, and this is a fair example of how to handle things in the aftermath of a bad product launch. But the whole situation—the bad publicity and the cost of the free goodies that had to be dispensed—could have been avoided by delaying the launch.

How to Handle an Offensive Social Remark

As a guy who has built up a pretty solid following based on fairly candid tweets, I speak from a position of authority when I say that social media can get you in a lot of trouble. I've also watched this phenomenon unfold, both as a paid PR professional and as an observer of social media trends.

The Justine Sacco incident is the most-well-known instance of someone making a stupid comment on social media, and I think it's going to stay that way for some time.

For those who never followed it, here's a recap. Sacco was a PR person for a company called InterActiveCorp (IAC), which owns the popular dating site Match.com, the influential website the Daily Beast, and a number of other well-known web properties. Sacco, who was born in South Africa, was on her way there when she sent out a tweet stating "Going to Africa. Hope I don't get AIDS. Just kidding. I'm white!" (http://www.nytimes.com/2015/02/15/magazine/how-one-stupid-tweet-ruined-justine-saccos-life.html?_r=0).

The kicker was that Sacco sent it before she got on her flight from London to South Africa, one of the longest non-stop commercial flights in the world. As Sacco was in transit, a massive campaign emerged on the Internet, condemning her tweet as a racist remark that trivialized the AIDS epidemic in Sub-Saharan Africa.

By the time Sacco landed, she had become the target of one of the most rapid (and, some would say, effective) public shaming campaigns on the Internet. Sacco lost her job and became a pariah, all because of one tweet. But not only was the content of her tweet reprehensible, she also showed a stunning lack of judgment, both as an individual and as an employee of a major web corporation.

Both IAC and Sacco issued statements in the wake of the public outcry. Let's take a look at them and go through what makes one effective and what makes the other a paltry, poor example of public relations. First, IAC's statement:

"There is no excuse for the hateful statements that have been made and we condemn them unequivocally. We hope, however, that time and action, and the forgiving human spirit, will not result in the wholesale condemnation of an individual who we have otherwise known to be a decent person at core" (http://www.adweek.com/adfreak/justine-sacco-fired-iac-hope-i-dont-get-aids-tweet-154639).

I give their response an 8 on a scale of 10. First and foremost, the company did the right thing and dismissed Sacco immediately. In the spy world, this is called a "burn notice," and it refers to the practice of disavowing an agent. In certain situations, there is a fine line between discipline and dismissal. I am not a moral compass, and I am not going to list every slur or comment that could or should get someone fired, but these are the basic ones that should get someone burned:

- Racism
- Sexism
- Homophobia
- Bigotry

In the event of those kinds of behavior, disavow. Burn them. This hardline attitude is necessary.

IAC's statement didn't say anything about Sacco, which I think is acceptable, but I would have thrown in something that condemned her behavior in unequivocal terms. Sacco had a history of offensive tweets, which was not really addressed in the statements that followed the incident. I have to admit that I very much respect any company willing to show some degree of warmth, though; they could have easily omitted the kind remark about her being a decent person.

Now, here's part of Sacco's statement:

"Words cannot express how sorry I am, and how necessary it is for me to apologize to the people of South Africa, who I have offended due to a needless and careless tweet. There is an AIDS crisis taking place in this country, that we read about in America, but do not live with or face on a continuous basis. Unfortunately, it is terribly easy to be cavalier about an epidemic that one has never witnessed firsthand."

The British judge (me) gives it a 1 out of 10.

Congratulations to Sacco for apologizing. Congratulations to her for recognizing that, yes, AIDS exists, there's an AIDS crisis in Africa, and Americans don't face it.

But she said nothing about how she would conduct herself in the future. She should have added, "I am going to seek help immediately." Why? Because it is *not* "terribly easy to be cavalier about AIDS," and she should figure out what was going on in her own mind before having a job interacting with the public again.

I'll be honest: I did feel some sympathy for Sacco. Being humiliated for her remarks is one thing. But receiving death threats (and other threats to one's physical safety) is wrong.

Sacco is the one who remains liable for her actions, and she's paid the price. If you are the sole person behind your product, then you ought to study the case of Justine Sacco and exercise some damn judgment when using social media. If you post offensive nonsense on your accounts, you need to remember that you are not a private citizen. You are representing your product, your brand, and your employees (god help them if you have any).

The challenge, of course, is to keep yourself and anyone who works for you feeling as though you can be candid and authentic and effective on social media (whether it's through humor, cutting insights, or tearing a strip off of people that are too high on themselves). The so-called third-rail topics I outlined above are a good place to start when drafting a policy on social media, and the apologies offered up by Sacco and the IAC are examples of when an apology doesn't quite cut it. It also helps to hire people who aren't thinking those things, but you're not a mind reader.

One of the more interesting elements of the public shaming that Sacco faced has to do with the idea that the Internet is a public record of everything you've ever said or done—and that these events don't disappear. Sacco's tweet, and the fallout from it, will likely follow her around for the rest of her life. Even if she does a complete 180 in how she thinks and acts, anytime someone Googles "Justine Sacco," the first result will be related to what happened in the past. One stupid tweet cost her her reputation and her entire online legacy. And as you'll see in our next case study, comments made in the past can easily end up biting you in the present.

Mere months before the popular photo-sharing app Snapchat was to decline a major round of fundraising from Facebook, emails written by founder and CEO Evan Spiegel emerged after languishing

for years in the catacombs of the Internet [http://valleywag.gawker
.com/fuck-bitches-get-leid-the-sleazy-frat-emails-of-snap-1582604137].
The emails dated back to Spiegel's fraternity days at Stanford
University. Like many young Ivy League men, he was full of arrogance
and bravado, and his emails displayed as much. The most famous
example was an email, related to a Hawaii-themed house party, that
used the phrase "fuck bitches, get leid" as a signoff.

Someone dug up the emails, which then made their way to a
number of blogs that cover the tech industry. As one might expect,
the reaction was swift and overwhelmingly negative. Spiegel issued
the following statement:

"I'm obviously mortified and embarrassed that my idiotic emails
during my fraternity days were made public. I have no excuse . . .
I'm sorry I wrote them at the time and I was [a] jerk to have written
them. They in no way reflect who I am today or my views towards
women."

I give Spiegel's approach to this situation a 4 out of 10. He can
be forgiven for being an idiot in college (or a jerk, as Spiegel called
himself), but to say nothing to the press beyond one vague statement
is utterly vapid. He took no further action, when he could have made
a donation to a relevant cause, announced an effort to police these
kinds of statements within Snapchat, or even discussed the issue
publicly in a more-open forum.

All we got from Spiegel is a long-winded version of "boys will
be boys." In my opinion, his saving grace was the fact that Snapchat
was gaining serious momentum and that there was little incentive
to remove him from the company. Sadly, dollars and cents won out
in this round, but the corporate culture of Snapchat will forever be
tainted by this incident.

Simply not saying inappropriate or offensive things and exercising good judgment when you are on the record can help you avoid being the instigator of an incident like Justine Sacco's Twitter catastrophe. But I also recognize that many of us were saying and doing things that ended up online before we knew that the web is a permanent record.

If you are faced with a situation like Spiegel's, don't just issue a statement full of platitudes and hope everyone forgets about it. Yes, you can stress that you were young and ignorant and immature enough to do these things, but your attitude needs a wholesale change if you are going to handle it effectively. Making yourself available to the media and being totally transparent in answering their questions will demonstrate that you are serious about making real changes. You want to stress who you have become in the years since you did those dumb things. Words are easy to spout off. Actions are the hard currency of behavior.

Better yet, in a few months' time, you could revisit the incident and show the world yet again how far you've come. Contrary to what you may think, this isn't mindlessly reopening old wounds. Instead, it's a way to strengthen your brand and demonstrate that you have the courage to be wrong, show contrition, and fix your mistakes.

Delays, Unforeseen Problems, Hacks, and Other Issues That Become Your Problem

In the first sub-chapter on defects, I offered up a bit of tough love for those who are facing a problem with their products: the issue may not be your fault, but it is your problem. The same is true of negative events that happen at a remove from your actual company.

At an emotional level, this seems totally unfair. You've done your job designing, engineering, testing, fundraising, and bringing your product to market. And now someone has completely undone all your hard work in a matter of seconds.

Sorry, but them's the breaks. A big part of leadership involves absorbing the blows that come with someone else screwing up. Why do you think chief executives and presidents of companies get paid so much? It's not *all* greed. Or work. Part of it is in recognition of the fact that they could be out of a job tomorrow if something catastrophic occurs and the company (and its shareholders) is negatively affected. An oil company CEO may make obscene amounts of money, but one big spill means that his company will suffer damage to its reputation and its finances for years to come, and he could be unemployable if he's let go in the aftermath.

As usual, honesty is the most effective strategy if something happens. You can and should be transparent about is what happening, but you also have to do it without appearing to point the finger at whatever third party is responsible.

Let's say that you've raised $100,000 on Kickstarter for a new wearable fitness device. You have promised that anybody who donates $1,000 or more will get a device for free, in an exclusive color and with some added features. You've managed to generate some pretty good buzz in the press, and even the established players are a little scared of what you've got coming.

As you're gearing up for the first production run, your sub-contractor in Asia tells you that, due to delays in sourcing a key component, you are going to blow your launch date. As a small upstart in a market dominated by major players, you cannot afford to have this happen. Fitness wearables are a hot item right now, and a delay could mean that your product is hitting the market at the tail end of the fad.

In this scenario, you can deal with the setback by not only being honest about what is going on but also being specific about when consumers can expect the problem to be fixed and when the product will launch. Even if it's an egregiously long time, like six months to a year, it's better to give that kind of timeline than nothing. Why?

Well, for one thing, so few people are willing to give anything more than a vague answer that a specific one looks good. It gives you the appearance of being in control, even when there's a crisis at hand. It will show that you're able to monitor and pinpoint the source of the problem and that you're able to bounce back. Not only is it refreshingly rare, but it demonstrates leadership and courage under fire, two traits that our society considers the apex of personal character.

A great solution here is to give weekly (heck, daily if you can) updates. The more, the better. The more specific, the better. Show manufacturing photos. Offer reporters the chance to visit the factory if they'd like. Show that you're holding yourself accountable to the product's existence as much as you can.

You really need to avoid and deflect the negative characterizations of you and your product, and stop one particularly dreaded label: *vaporware* is used to describe products that are consistently promised but fail to materialize. Even when a product labeled this way does emerge, the term is practically a death sentence. Expectations will always be heightened due to the pent-up demand, and the product rarely ever meets them. When it doesn't, the "vaporware" label can be invoked as yet another point of criticism ("We waited X number of years for *this* piece of crap?"). Either way, it's bad news for you and your product.

Data breaches are another area in which there's a delicate balance between remaining transparent and maintaining a certain level of confidentiality. On one hand, you may not be able to divulge everything, so as not to compromise an ongoing investigation. On the other hand, people tend to freak out when their personal and financial data gets out in the open, and rightly so. It's a testy situation, and in many cases you may not completely understand it yourself; you may be a CEO, but you are not necessarily an expert in computers, hacking, or really anything technical. As a result, it can be quite scary to comment.

The appropriate legal authorities—whether it's your legal team, the police, or government entities—will have advice for you. Some of these hacks, like the one that hit a couple of major big box stores a few years back, are the result of sophisticated international hackers who have motives beyond just stealing some credit-card numbers so they can sign up for paid porn sites. In those instances, you'll be dealing with serious government organizations, and you don't want to blow up their work *or* spook your customers unnecessarily.

But as a PR person, I feel an obligation to urge you, as a good business practice, to be as open as possible in that situation. If nothing else, you owe it to your customers to reassure them of your commitment to the safety of their data. At the *very* least, you should say that you will, as I've already advised, give regular updates on the situation.

So what to do then? First of all, don't lie. If you've read this far, you know that lying only comes back to haunt you. Do you want to be known as the merchant who has shitty payment-processing systems and then lies to their customers about it? Yeah, I thought not. You also can't afford to sit on your hands and say nothing or try to deflect attention away from the situation. Consumers are extremely sensitive when it comes to anything financial.

So with that in mind, you can start here:

1. Apologize. This is a no-brainer, and make sure it is a heartfelt, sincere apology, not just typical boilerplate.

2. Let them know what steps you are taking to resolve the matter. If you really are the victim of hacking and the FBI is investigating what happened, then tell your customers everything you can—except that which could compromise the work of law enforcement. Hearing that they've been hacked isn't going to brighten your customers' day, but knowing that both you and the relevant authorities are doing something about it will at least reassure them that someone is looking out for their interests.

3. Do something about it. Tangible action in the wake of a crisis beats a nicely worded statement every time. One thing you can do that won't cost you anything is to facilitate communication between the customers and the payment processor or the credit card company. Your customers will go through a fair amount of hassle in dealing with all the anti-fraud departments and procedures. If there's anything you can do to smooth it over, then do it. Second, you can and should offer some kind of token: credit for your products, gift cards, a hand-delivered note thanking customers for their continued patronage. A small gesture like that will go a long way toward soothing any flaring tempers regarding the incident.

How Did That Leak Get Out There?

Before I speak any further, I should add that I am in no way a lawyer, nor does this constitute legal advice. You should get real legal advice when dealing with this sort of situation.

With that in mind, the best defense is to have a clearly defined policy about internal communications. It should not sound like jargon-laced corporate bullshit. You and your organization should treat all communications—whether it's email, texts, or a message in Slack or WhatsApp—as if they can and will be displayed on a Jumbotron in Times Square.

Remind everybody on a monthly basis of this policy. If you hear them groaning, say, "I know it's repetitive," but tell them how important it is that they remember it as part of their ongoing routine.

Let them know that although it's unreasonable to expect that everything they say be public-friendly—you will have to discuss new clients, new business, new money, bad employees, bad situations—you want to eliminate the chance that they could say something that would get them lambasted in the press or even sent to jail. There's a reason that financial firms hire compliance professionals, many of whom are lawyers, to sit around and monitor internal communications, and it's not to find out which employees are screwing each other outside work hours.

In the event that you are confronted with the leak, say one thing and one thing only: "I will get back to you ASAP once I know more about what you have shown me." Be careful with your wording. I also recommend you don't immediately copy your lawyer on the email. Just say something along the lines of, "I have seen this email from you, and the moment I know more I will get back to you and tell you what I can." If the person in question gets confrontational, you can say, "I don't know more than what you've shown me, and I'm not trying to dodge your questions; I want to give an answer." If they keep emailing, ignore it.

Until you, yourself, have confirmed that the leak exists, that it is real, that they have not fabricated it, and that it is not a trick or a trap, you do not want to be the person confirming that it exists.

If your leaked emails are taken wildly out of context and result in a story that is verifiably false, then you can adopt a different strategy. But this is effective only if you can prove, categorically, that this situation is not true, that the person leveling these accusations is incorrect, and that it's all nonsense. You should be *very* sure of that, because if you lay the hammer down and get proven wrong (or later change your tune), you will look very silly. Just remember the lesson of Mr. Morin and his "we don't keep your data" routine.

If you come across some kind of false accusation, then you can and should provide as much detail as possible to show why it's not true. If you are limited in the level of evidence you can give, under either legal counsel or an ongoing investigation, then be brief and explain why your comments are limited at the current moment. If you want, you can ask to show the evidence off the record or under some sort of legal disclosure that ensures the person will be unable to show it beyond the editorial staffers who actively police such things. The point here isn't to hide the truth; it's to protect trade secrets.

Leaks may be the result of someone who has an axe to grind trying to make you look bad. If this is the case, then by all means, bury them—but do it properly. That means no bad language, no swearing, and no taunting on social media. When you're asked to comment, explain the situation calmly and forthrightly. Don't even address the person who said it; address the situation and the content.

Maybe an employee is trying to say that you owe them money, and leaking emails is a way to get you to pay up. Obviously, if you do owe them, then pay them; you should never have let it get that far. If you have good reasons for doing so and your lawyer thinks it won't leave you open to further complications, it may be worth sharing the emails. Money problems? Say you had money problems. Confusion over the payment terms? Talk about that. It may be as simple as saying those things and being a real person who doesn't suck, to make the situation go away.

If they're full of crap and using it as a means of extortion, then you have my permission to lay it all out in the open. Tell the world, in an adult manner, that this is a disgruntled employee and they're trying to make you look bad on the public stage. Always, however, do a cost-benefit evaluation. If someone with a powerful reputation wants to battle it out in the media or bring you down in the press, you may want to handle it quietly *and hold them to a binding non-disclosure agreement.* Yes, you could call that extortion. I call it a sad, annoying marketing expense.

If you're ready to go to war, explain why they are in the wrong, and use only the facts, not your opinions or interpretations. This is the intelligent, tactical approach to dealing with what is essentially a person hoping to annoy you into a particular course of action. What you may not realize (especially under pressure in the heat of the moment) is that this is the course of action taken by powerless people. I am a big proponent of always telling the truth, and it's for a good reason: *the truth always wins.* There may be some uncomfortable moments when you're first facing this kind of situation, but in the end, honesty always wins out—and your accuser will have to face the blow to their reputation that comes with being known for using underhanded and dishonest tactics to get their way. If your soul is clean, you didn't do anything wrong, and this person is causing you harm because they *can* and because they *want money*, then show them what's what.

Further Leakages

Another arena where a leak may occur is in the realm of office romances. Most workplaces forbid these kinds of relationships or at least heavily discourage them, for very obvious reasons. If the relationship sours, then the entire office can be impacted by the interpersonal drama of two people. You'll have to decide for yourself how you want to handle these situations, but from a PR perspective, there are two possible outcomes regarding a leak of this nature.

1. If a leak involving a consensual interoffice tryst is publicized and there is no infidelity involved, then there is no story. It's gossip, and you can say, "This is a personal matter internal to the company." End of story.
    a. Here's a caveat. If one of the people is an executive or someone in a seat of power and the other person isn't, this can be extremely negative. Even if it's perfectly consensual, the questions people may ask about the relationship, even if it doesn't go sour, could make your other employees question the fairness of the company.
    b. If this leads to any kind of special treatment that becomes public, you are in a lot of deep, stinky doo-doo, and I recommend you monitor the situation internally as best as possible. If any uneven treatment occurs, deal with it swiftly.
        i. You may even want to consider telling the press about it before anyone else can. It depends on the egregiousness of the situation. Better that you leak it than a disgruntled employee does. However, this isn't a book about internal relations.

2. There is some kind of questionable behavior involved: infidelity, nonconsensual conduct, threats, stalking, or any behavior that could involve law enforcement. This only becomes more awful if an executive is involved.

In 2014, Tinder's former VP of marketing Whitney Wolfe broke up with her boyfriend Justin Mateen, Tinder's CMO and co-founder [http://valleywag.gawker.com/ex-vp-sues-tinder-alleging-coworker-called-her-a-whore-1598345367]. A series of texts between Mateen and Wolfe were leaked, showing Mateen engaging in egregiously bad behavior. In addition to the typical wounded lover behavior, he directed threats and slurs against Wolfe and others. A sexual harassment lawsuit followed, with Wolfe claiming that she was dismissed from the company because of Mateen's abuse.

The parties settled the lawsuit out of court. Legally, the matter is over, but we can still learn a lesson or two from this.

This incident has all the nasty elements of a perfect PR storm wrapped into one: anger, jealousy, racism, hurt feelings, sexism, and public embarrassment. It's the kind of situation that would make you want to crawl into a hole and die if it were going on at your company. It led to Sean Rad, the CEO, eventually exiting Tinder [http://techcrunch.com/2014/11/04/tinders-sean-rad-demoted-from-ceo-will-serve-as-president-of-board/].

It's also an example of a crucial time to practice internal PR as well as external PR.

This kind of behavior *cannot be tolerated*. Any kind of harassment is unacceptable in the workplace, for the sake of your corporate culture and your employees. In the Tinder case, Mateen left the company only after the lawsuit was settled [http://www.latimes.com/

business/technology/la-fi-tn-tinder-whitney-wolfe-20140908-story .html]. In my view, retaining somebody you know has acted in a hostile manner toward another employee sets a precedent for future behavior. It's a tacit admission that some people can get away with reprehensible behavior and that harassment will be tolerated within the company.

Other situations are less black and white. Telling the public (and your own people) that you are investigating the situation is the smart thing to do. Silence will lead only to speculation that you are dodging the issue or trying to make it go away. However, in the Tinder case, reacting in a cold and emotionless manner to the texts may have also been a mistake. The texts were damning and the content vile. Nobody at Tinder said that. You don't even have to admit that they exist to say, "The type of content we have seen reported is disgusting." That's called being a human.

If you have solid evidence that there was wrongdoing—the kind that would hold up in court and that you know is not misrepresented—then you have my complete permission to throw the offender under the bus. Dismiss them with extreme prejudice. Release an unequivocal statement stating that you will not tolerate that kind of behavior from an employee and that they are no longer with the company. If the victim is a woman (and they tend to be on the receiving end in these situations), then let everyone know that your company is a safe place for women to work.

What really got me angry about the incident was the internal memo released by Sean Rad. Although Rad affirmed Tinder's commitment to gender equality in the workplace, he still managed to insert this bit into the statement:

"Whitney's legal complaint is full of factual inaccuracies and omissions. We did not discriminate against Whitney because of her age or gender, and her complaint paints an inaccurate picture of my actions and what went on here."

If there were ever a classless, passive-aggressive way to try to discredit someone making serious allegations against an employee of your company, this is it. The accuracy of the legal complaint is irrelevant here. It's a matter before the courts, and it should be decided in that setting. All Rad had to do was condemn the behavior, state that it was under investigation, and say that further comment would follow. No cheap shots needed.

When Words and Actions Go Too Far

A lot of what we've focused on involves what people *say*, particularly on public forums like social media. You're more likely to be dealing with what people say rather than actions they take, but the stakes are roughly equal, no matter what happens.

Never, ever attempt to explain away a racist, sexist, or otherwise prejudiced statement in a vague manner. It is not your job to explain why they said it, nor is there *any excuse* for racism, sexism, homophobia, or any other form of discrimination. It is my opinion that any individual making those statements in the context of professional communications should seek professional help and take real action to find out what led them to do so. In nearly all cases, I would terminate the offender immediately—and not just to make an example out of them or redeem my organization in the eyes of the public.

I realize that, on the surface, this may seem like an extreme reaction. But public relations is about more than just your reputation in the world. Good PR also helps manage your internal reputation, including the way your employees feel about your organization and the culture that prevails within it. In a way, this is even more important than trying to save your ass after someone runs their mouth off. If your people think that you will give somebody a pass even after they've said or done something horrible, then it will inevitably lead to morale problems. Your employees will start to think about your organization as a toxic place where transgressions are left unpunished. This is especially true as the disparity in pay among genders and races becomes more and more obvious.

Being drunk or angry is no excuse, either. In fact, it only raises the stakes. Not only do you have to address the issue of discrimination, but there's now a mental-health or addiction component to it. This requires a delicate mixture of justice and compassion. The behavior at hand could be the symptom of a deeper problem, and for both internal and external reasons, you will have to plumb the depths of your emotional and logical faculties. It's one thing if the person goes on a swearing tirade about another company. That's perhaps where you say, "This person's going through a lot, and we're going to help them through it." It's another if they're saying horrific word-crimes about the person in question's sex, gender, or race. In that case, kick them to the curb.

A situation like that will be a true test of your leadership in both the internal and external realms. On the one hand, you cannot excuse the behavior. But you also can't be unsympathetic to those kinds of issues when they arise. Someone in your organization may see a harsh reaction as a reason to hide their own issues, and that leads to its own toxic spillover into the workplace. You cannot compel somebody to seek help for addiction or depression or any other mental illness unless they are ready and willing to do so. But at the same time, letting their issues affect your organization isn't something you are required to tolerate. Disclosing a condition is completely at the discretion of the person affected, but if it's known within the company but not externally, you should let it be known that although their condition is a terrible burden for them to bear, it is impacting the culture of your company too much and it is best to part ways. I have both the inattentive type of attention deficit hyperactivity disorder (ADHD) and an anxiety disorder. One company I worked for specifically took me aside and talked to me about them, asked how the conditions and my workplace affected me, and worked with me in a subtle and caring manner. It meant the world to me.

And while I choose to treat addiction as a mental health issue rather than a criminal one, you can draw a clear line at criminal behavior. Being an alcoholic is not the same thing as being arrested for driving while intoxicated. More serious charges, like domestic abuse and cruelty to animals, will cast a long shadow over your organization. There is nothing you can do but condemn the behavior in the strongest terms and part ways with the offender. Don't even think about it from a PR perspective. It's simply a matter of whether you, as a leader, will stand for that kind of behavior, for having someone who will commit those acts be a part of what you've built. I can't imagine why the answer would be anything but no.

conclusion

If my last book was a letter I wanted to send back in time to my younger self, this book is what I want to hand to anyone who wants to understand public relations in its present form. That doesn't mean it's a textbook or an explanation of everything that could possibly happen in the industry. Most PR firms fall flat on their face when asked to do this kind of work—hopefully I've given you the tools required to succeed.

If you're an agency person who simply doesn't want to be good and who wants to continue to re-grow the industry scabs of bad PR, I am coming for you. You aren't part of a dying breed yet, but if I have anything to do with it, you will be.

Finally, if you read this and felt a pang of sadness, knowing that you've been had, I'm sorry.

Whoever you are, I hope you learned *something* from this. The world could use more people who understand that being popular doesn't mean being a liar, that being famous doesn't mean crushing others on the way to the top, and that being a public figure doesn't require a lot of nonsense.

If you ever want to talk, my email is ed@ezpr.com.

CPSIA information can be obtained
at www.ICGtesting.com
Printed in the USA
BVHW050443190523
664429BV00011B/283